Photo *N. Y. Herald*

WARREN GAMALIEL HARDING

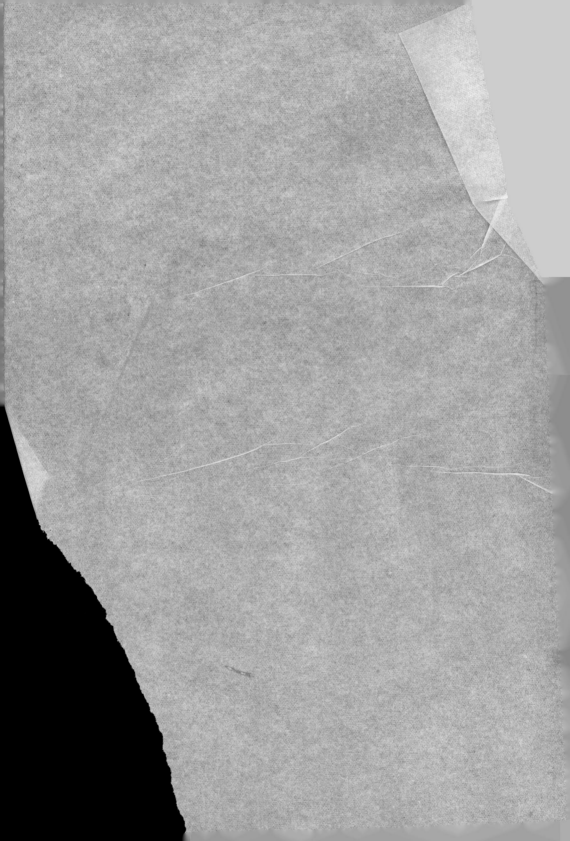

THE MIRRORS OF WASHINGTON

ANONYMOUS

With Fourteen Cartoons by
CESARE
and Fourteen Portraits

G. P. PUTNAM'S SONS
NEW YORK AND LONDON
The Knickerbocker Press
1921

CONTENTS

WITH BIOGRAPHICAL NOTES

CONTENTS

HARVEY, George (Brinton McClellan),

Editor; b. Peacham, Vt., Feb. 16, 1864; Educ.
Peacham Academy; (LL.D., University of Nevada, University of Vermont, Middlebury Coll.
and Erskine Coll.). Consecutively reporter
Springfield *Republican*, Chicago *News*, and New
York *World*, 1882–6; ins. commr. of N. J., 1890–1;
mng. editor New York *World*, 1891–93; con-
structor and pres. various electric railroads, 1894–
8; purchased, 1899, and since editor *North Ameri-
can Review*, Pres. Harper & Bros., 1900–15; North
Am. Review Pub. Co., 1899– ; editor and pub.
Harvey's *Weekly;* dir. Audit Co. of New York;
Col. and a.-d.-c. on staffs of Govs. Green and
Abbett, of N. J., 1885–92; hon. col. and a.-d.-c. on
staffs of Govs. Heyward and Ansel, of S. C.; U. S.
Ambassador to Court of Saint James . . **49**

HUGHES, Charles Evans,

Secretary of State; b. at Glens Falls, N. Y., Apr. 11,
1862; Educ. Colgate U., 1876–8; A.B., Brown U.,

CONTENTS

CONTENTS

HOOVER, Herbert Clark,

Secretary of Commerce; Engineer; b. West Branch, Ia.,
Aug. 10, 1874; Educ. B.A. (in mining engring.), Le-
land Stanford, Jr., U., 1895; (LL.D., Brown U., U.
of Pa., Harvard, Princeton, Yale, Oberlin, U. of Ala.,
Liège, Brussels; D.C.L., Oxford); Asst. Ark. Geol.
Survey, 1893, U. S. Geol. Survey, Sierra Nevada
Mountains, 1895; in W. Australia as chief of mining
staff of Bewick, Moreing & Co. and mgr. Han-
nan's Brown Hill Mine, 1897; chief engr. Chinese
Imperial Bur. of Mines, 1899, doing extensive
exploration in interior of China. Took part in
defense of Tientsin during Boxer disturbances;
Chmn. Am. Relief Com. London, 1914–15,
Commn. for Relief in Belgium, 1915–18; chmn.
food com. Council of Nat. Defense, Apr.-Aug.
1917; apptd. U. S. food administrator by President
Wilson, Aug. 10, 1917, resigned June, 1919.

LODGE, Henry Cabot,

Senator; b. Boston, May 12, 1850; Educ. A.B., Har-
vard, 1871, LL.B., 1875, Ph.D. (history), 1876;
(LL.D., Williams, 1893, Yale, 1902, Clark U.,
1902, Harvard, 1904, Amherst, 1912, also Union
Col., Princeton U., and Dartmouth Coll., and
Brown, 1918); Admitted to bar, 1876; editor *North
American Review*, 1873–6, *International Review*,
1879–81; mem. Mass. Ho. of Rep., 1880, 81; mem.

CONTENTS

CONTENTS

CONTENTS

CONTENTS

ILLUSTRATIONS

THE MIRRORS OF
WASHINGTON

WARREN GAMALIEL HARDING

EVERY time we elect a new President we learn what a various creature is the Typical American.

When Mr. Roosevelt was in the White House the Typical American was gay, robustious, full of the joy of living, an expansive spirit from the frontier, a picaresque twentieth century middle class Cavalier. He hit the line hard and did not flinch. And his laugh shook the skies.

Came Wilson. And the Typical American was troubled about his soul. Rooted firmly in the church-going past, he carried the banner of the Lord, Democracy, idealistic, bent on perfecting that old incorrigible Man, he cuts off the right hand that offends him and votes for prohibition and woman suffrage, a Round Head in a Ford.

Eight years and we have the perfectly typical American, Warren Gamaliel Harding of the modern type, the Square Head, typical of that America whose artistic taste is the movies, who reads and

finds mental satisfaction in the vague inanities of
the small town newspaper, who has faith in America, who is for liberty, virtue, happiness, prosperity,
law and order and all the standard generalities and
holds them a perfect creed; who distrusts anything
new except mechanical inventions, the standardized product of the syndicate which supplies his
nursing bottle, his school books, his information,
his humor in a strip, his art on a screen, with a
quantity production mind, cautious, uniformly
hating divergence from uniformity, jailing it in
troublous times, prosperous, who has his car and
his bank account and can sell a bill of goods as well
as the best of them.

People who insist upon having their politics
logical demand to know the why of Harding. Why
was a man of so undistinguished a record as he
first chosen as a candidate for President and then
elected President?

As a legislator he had left no mark on legislation.
If he had retired from Congress at the end of his
term his name would have existed only in the old
Congressional directories, like that of a thousand
others. As a public speaker he had said nothing
that anybody could remember. He had passed
through a Great War and left no mark on it. He

had shared in a fierce debate upon the peace that
followed the war but though you can recall small
persons like McCumber and Kellogg and Moses
and McCormick in that discussion you do not
recall Harding. To be sure he made a speech in
that debate which he himself says was a great
speech but no newspaper thought fit to publish it
because of its quality, or felt impelled to publish
it in spite of its quality because it had been made
by Harding.

He neither compelled attention by what he said
nor by his personality. Why, then, without fire-
works, without distinction of any sort, without
catching the public eye, or especially deserving to
catch it, was Warren Harding elected President of
the United States?

One plausible reason why he was nominated was
that given by Senator Brandegee at Chicago,
where he had a great deal to do with the nomination. "There ain't any first raters this year. This
ain't any 1880 or any 1904. We haven't any John
Shermans or Theodore Roosevelts. We've got
a lot of second raters and Warren Harding is the
best of the second raters."

Once nominated as a Republican his election of
course inevitably followed. But to accept Mr.

Brandegee's plea in avoidance is to agree to the eternal poverty of American political life, for most of our presidents have been precisely like Warren G. Harding, first-class second raters.

Mrs. Harding, a woman of sound sense and much energy had an excellent instructive answer to the "why." The pictures of the house in Marion, the celebrated front porch, herself and her husband were taken to be exhibited by cinema all over the land. She said, "I want the people to see these pictures so that they will know we are just folks like themselves."

Warren Harding is "just folks." A witty woman said of him, alluding to the small town novel which was popular at the time of his inauguration, "Main Street has arrived in the White House."

The Average Man has risen up and by seven million majority elected an Average Man President. His defects were his virtues. He was chosen rather for what he wasn't than for what he was,— the inconspicuousness of his achievements. The "just folks" level of his mind, his small town man's caution, his sense of the security of the past, his average hopes and fears and practicality, his standardized Americanism which would enable a people

who wanted for a season to do so to take themselves
politically for granted.

The country was tired of the high thinking and
rather plain spiritual living of Woodrow Wilson.
It desired the man in the White House to cause it
no more moral overstrain than does the man you
meet in the Pullman smoking compartment or the
man who writes the captions for the movies who
employs a sort of Inaugural style, freed from the
inhibitions of statesmanship. It was in a mood
similar to that of Mr. Harding himself when after
his election he took Senators Freylinghuysen, Hale,
and Elkins with him on his trip to Texas. Senator
Knox observing his choice is reported to have said,
"I think he is taking those three along because he
wanted complete mental relaxation." All his life
Mr. Harding has shown a predilection for companions who give him complete mental relaxation,
though duty compels him to associate with the
Hughes and the Hoovers. The conflict between
duty and complete mental relaxation establishes a
strong bond of sympathy between him and the
average American.

The "why" of Harding is the democratic passion
for equality. We are standardized, turned out like
Fords by the hundred million, and we cannot en-

dure for long anyone who is not standardized.
Such an one casts reflections upon us; why should
we by our votes unnecessarily asperse ourselves?
Occasionally we may indulge nationally, as men do
individually, in the romantic belief that we are
somebody else, that we are like Roosevelt or Wilson—and they become typical of what we would be
—but always we come back to the knowledge that
we are nationally like Harding, who is typical of
what we are. "Just folks" Kuppenheimered,
movieized, associated pressed folks.

Men debate whether or not Mr. Wilson was a
great man and they will keep on doing so until the
last of those passes away whose judgment of him
is clouded by the sense of his personality. But
men will never debate about the greatness of Mr.
Harding, not even Mr. Harding himself. He is
modest. He has only two vanities, his vanity
about his personal appearance and his vanity about
his literary style.

The inhibitions of a presidential candidate,
bound to speak and say nothing, irked him.

"Of course I could make better speeches than
these" he told a friend during the campaign, "but
I have to be so careful."

In his inaugural address he let himself go, as

8

much as it is possible for a man so cautious as he is to let himself go. It was a great speech, an inaugural to place alongside the inaugurals of Lincoln and Washington, written in his most capable English, Harding at his best. It is hard for a man to move Marion for years with big editorials, to receive the daily compliments of Dick Cressinger and Jim Prendergast, without becoming vain of the power of his pen. It is his chief vanity and it is one that it is hard for him who speaks or writes to escape. He has none of that egotism which makes a self-confident man think himself the favorite of fortune.

He said after his nomination at Chicago, "We drew to a pair of deuces and filled." He did not say it boastfully as a man who likes to draw to a pair of deuces and who always expects to fill. He said it with surprise and relief. He does not like to hold a pair of deuces and be forced to draw to them. He has not a large way of regarding losing and winning as all a part of the game. He hates to lose. He hated to lose even a friendly game of billiards in the Marion Club with his old friend Colonel Christian, father of his secretary, though the stake was only a cigar.

When he was urged to seek the Republican

nomination for the Presidency he is reported to have said, "Why should I. My chances of winning are not good. If I let you use my name I shall probably in the end lose the nomination for the Senate. (His term was expiring.) If I don't run for the Presidency I can stay in the Senate all my life. I like the Senate. It is a very pleasant place."

The Senate is like Marion, Ohio, a very pleasant place, for a certain temperament. And Mr. Harding stayed in Marion all his life until force—a vis exterior; there is nothing inside Mr. Harding that urges him on and on—until force of circumstances, of politics, of other men's ambitions, took him out of Marion and set him down in Washington, in the Senate.

The process of uprooting him from the pleasant place of Marion is reported to have been thus described by his political transplanter, the present Attorney General, Mr. Daugherty: "When it came to running for the Senate I found him, sunning himself in Florida, like a turtle on a log and I had to push him into the water and make him swim."

And a similar thing happened when it came to running for the Presidency. It is a definite type of man who suns himself on a log, who is seduced by pleasant places like Marion, Ohio, whom the big town does not draw into its magnetic field, whose heart is not excited by the larger chances of life. Is he lazy? Is he lacking in imagination? Does he hate to lose? Does he want self-confidence? Is he over modest? Has he no love for life, life as a great adventure? Whatever he is, Mr. Harding is that kind of man, that kind of man to start out with.

But this is only the point of departure, that choice to remain in a pleasant place like Marion, not to risk what you have, your sure place in society as the son of one of the better families, the reasonable prospect that the growth of your small town will bring some accretion to your own fortunes, the decision not to hazard greatly in New York or Chicago or on the frontier. Life asks little of you in those pleasant places like Marion and in return for that little gives generously, especially if you are, to begin with, well placed, if you are ingratiatingly handsome, if your personality is agreeable—"The best fellow in the world to play poker with all Saturday night," as a Marionite feelingly described the President to me, and if you have a gift of words as handsome and abundant as your looks.

Mr. Harding is a handsome man, endowed with

the gifts that reinforce the charm of his exterior, a
fine voice, a winning smile, a fluency of which his
inaugural is the best instance; an ample man, you
might say. But he is too handsome, too endowed,
for his own good, his own spiritual good. The
slight stoop of his shoulders, the soft figure, the
heaviness under the eyes betray in some measure
perhaps the consequences of nature's excessive
generosity. Given all these things you take, it
may be, too much for granted. There is not much
to stiffen the mental, moral, and physical fibers.

Given such good looks, such favor from nature,
and an environment in which the struggle is not
sharp and existence is a species of mildly purpose-
ful flanerie. You lounge a bit stoop-shoulderedly
forward to success. There is nothing hard about
the President. I once described him in somewhat
this fashion to a banker in New York who was interested in knowing what kind of a President we
had.

"You agree," he said, "with a friend of Harding's who came in to see me a few days ago. This
friend said to me 'Warren is the best fellow in the
world. He has wonderful tact. He knows how to
make men work with him and how to get the best
out of them. He is politically adroit. He is con-

scientious. He has a keen sense of his responsibilities. He has unusual common sense.' And he named other similar virtues, 'Well,' I asked him, 'What is his defect?' 'Oh,' he replied, 'the only trouble with Warren is that he lacks mentality.'"

The story, like most stories, exaggerates. The President has the average man's virtues of common sense and conscientiousness with rather more than the average man's political skill and the average man's industry or lack of industry. His mentality is not lacking; it is undisciplined, especially in its higher ranges, by hard effort. There is a certain softness about him mentally. It is not an accident that his favorite companions are the least intellectual members of that house of average intelligence, the Senate. They remind him of the mental surroundings of Marion, the pleasant but unstimulating mental atmosphere of the Marion Club, with its successful small town business men, its local store-keepers, its banker whose mental horizon is bounded by Marion County, the value of whose farm lands for mortgages he knows to a penny, the lumber dealer whose eye rests on the forests of Kentucky and West Virginia.

The President has never felt the sharpening of competition. He was a local pundit because he was the editor. He was the editor because he owned the Republican paper of Marion. There was no effective rival. No strong intelligence challenged his and made him fight for his place. He never studied hard or thought deeply on public questions. A man who stays where he is put by birth tends to accept authority, and authority is strong in small places. The acceptance of authority implies few risks. It is like staying in Marion instead of going to New York or even Cleveland. It is easier, and often more profitable than studying hard or thinking deeply or inquiring too much.

And Mr. Harding's is a mind that bows to authority. What his party says is enough for Mr. Harding. His party is for protection and Mr. Harding is for protection; the arguments for protection may be readily assimilated from the editorials of one good big city newspaper and from a few campaign addresses. His party is for the remission of tolls on American shipping in the Panama Canal and Mr. Harding is for the remission of tolls. Mr. Root broke with his party on tolls and Mr. Harding is as much shocked at Mr. Root's deviation as the matrons of Marion would be over the public disregard of the Seventh Commandment by one of their number. His party became somehow for the payment of Colombia's Panama claims and Mr. Harding was for their payment.

A story tells just how Senator Kellogg went to the President to oppose the Colombia treaty. After hearing Mr. Kellogg Mr. Harding remarked, "Well, Frank, you have something on me. You've evidently read the treaty. I haven't."

A mind accepting authority favors certain general policies. It is not sufficiently inquiring to trouble itself with the details. Mr. Harding is for all sorts of things but is content to be merely for them. A curious illustration developed in Marion, during the visits of the best minds. He said to the newspaper men there one day, "I am for voluntary military training."

"What would you train, Mr. President," asked one of the journalists, "officers or men?"

The President hesitated. At last he said, "I haven't thought of that."

"But," said one of his interlocutors, "the colleges are training a lot of officers now."

This brought no response.

Another who had experience in the Great War remarked, "In the last war we were lacking in trained non-coms; it would be a good idea to train a lot of them."

"Yes," rejoined Mr. Harding eagerly, "That would be a good idea."

A more inquiring mind would have gone further than to be "for voluntary military training." A quicker, less cautious, if no more thorough mind would have answered the first question, "What would you train, officers or men?" by answering instantly "Both."

In that colloquy you have revealed all the mental habits of Mr. Harding. He was asked once, after he had had several conferences with Senator McCumber, Senator Smoot, Representative Fordney, and others who would be responsible for financial legislation, "Have you worked out the larger details of your taxation policy?"

"Naturally not!" was his reply. That "naturally" sprang I suppose from his habit of believing that somewhere there is authority. Somewhere there would be authority to determine what the larger details of the party's financial policy should be.

Now, this authority is not going to be any one man or any two men. The President, his friends tell us, is jealous of any assumption of power by any of his advisers. He is unwilling to have the public think that any other than himself is President. A man as handsome as Harding, as vain of his literary style as he is, has an ego that is not capable of total self-effacement. He will bow to impersonal authority like that of the party, or invoke the anonymous governance of "best minds," calling rather often on God as a well established authority, but he will not let authority be personal and be called Daugherty, or Lodge or Knox or whomever you will.

The President's attitude is rather like that of the average man during the campaign. If you said to a voter on a Pullman, "Mr. Harding is a man of small public experience, not known by any large political accomplishment," he would always answer optimistically, "Well, they will see to it that he makes good." Asked who "They" were he was always vague and elusive, gods on the mountain perhaps. There is an American religion, the average man's faith: it is "Them." "They" are the fountain of authority.

As Mr. Harding knew little competition in Marion so he has known little competition in public life which in this country is not genuinely competitive. Mr. Lloyd George is at the head of the British government because he is the greatest master of the House of Commons in a generation and he is chosen by the men who know him for what he is, his fellow members of the House of Commons. An American President is selected by the newspapers, which know little about him, by the politicians, who do not want a master but a slave, by the delegates to a national convention, tired, with hotel bills mounting, ready to name anybody in order to go home. The presidency, the one great prize in American public life, is attained by no known rules and under conditions which have nothing in them to make a man work hard or think hard, especially one endowed with a handsome face and figure, an ingratiating personality, and a literary style.

The small town man, unimaginative and of restricted mental horizon does not think in terms of masses of mankind. Masses vaguely appall him. They exist in the big cities on which he turned his back in his unaudacious youth. His contacts are with individuals. His democracy consists in smiling upon the village painter and calling him "Harry," in always nodding to the village cobbler and calling him "Bill," in stopping on the street corner with a group, which has not been invited to join the village club, putting his hand on the shoulder of one of them and calling them "Fellows."

Politics in the small town is limited to dealing with persons, to enlisting the support of men with a following at the polls.

Mr. Harding once drew this picture of his idea of politics. "If I had a policy to put over I should go about it this way," he said. "You all know the town meeting, if not by experience, by hearsay. Now if I had a program that I wanted to have adopted by a town meeting I should go to the three or four most influential men in my community. I should talk it out with them. I should make concessions to them until I had got them to agree with me. And then I should go into the town meeting feeling perfectly confident that my plan would go through. Well it's the same in the nation as in the town meeting, or in the whole world, if you will. I should always go first to the three or four leading men."

Mr. Harding thinks of politics in this personal way. He does not conceive of it as the force of ideas or the weight of morality moving the hearts of mankind. Mankind is only a word to him, one that he often uses,—or perhaps he prefers humanity, which has two more syllables—a large loose word that he employs to make his thought look bigger than it really is, something like the stage device for making an ordinary man seem ten feet tall.

Thus he will never try to move the mass of the people as his predecessors have. He will not "go to the country." He will not bring public opinion to bear as a disciplinary force in his household. He will treat the whole United States as if it were a Marion, consulting endless "best minds," composing differences, seeking unity, with the aid of his exceptional tact.

This attitude has its disadvantages. If you have a passion for ideas and an indifference for persons you can say "yes" or "no" easily; you may end by being dictatorial and arrogant, as Mr. Wilson was; but you will not be weak. If, on the contrary, you are indifferent to ideas and considerate of persons you find it hard to say "Decided" to any question. And somewhere there must be authority, the passing of the final judgment and the giving of orders.

But he compensates for his own defects. Almost as good as greatness is a knowledge of your own limitations; and Mr. Harding knows his thoroughly. Out of his modesty, his desire to reinforce himself, has proceeded the strongest cabinet that Washington has seen in a generation. He likes to have decisions rest upon the broad base of more than one intelligence and he has surrounded himself for this purpose with able associates. His policies will lack imagination, which is not a composite product, but they will have practicality, which is the greatest common denomination of several minds; and he, moreover, is himself unimaginative and practical.

Whatever superstructure of world organization he takes part in, behind it will be the reality, a private understanding with the biggest man in sight; for this reason the fall of Lloyd George and the succession of a Labor government in England will disconcert him terribly. The democratic passion for equality, which dogs the tracks of the great, he mollifies by reminding the nation always that he is "just folks," by opening the White House lawn gates, by calling everyone by his first name. So constant is his aim to appease it that I wonder if he is not sometimes betrayed into addressing his Secretary of State as "Charley."

WOODROW WILSON

WOODROW WILSON

THE explanation of President Wilson will be found in a certain inferiority. When all his personal history becomes known, when his papers and letters have all been published and read, when the memoirs of others have told all that there is to be told, there will stand clear something inadequate, a lack of robustness, mental or nervous, an excessive sensitiveness, over self-consciousness, shrinking from life, a neurotic something that in the end brought on defeat and the final overthrow. He was never quite a normal man with the average man's capacity to endure and enjoy but a strange, impeded, self-absorbed personality.

History arranged the greatest stage of all time, and on it placed a lot of little figures, "pigmy minds"—all save one, and he the nearest great, an unworldly person summoned from a cloister, with the vision of genius and the practical incapacity of one who has run away from life, hating men but loving all mankind, eloquent but inarticulate in a large way, incapable of true self expression in his chosen field of political action, so self-centered that he forgot the world's tragedy and merged it into his own, making great things little and little things great, one of "life's ironies," the everlasting refutation of the optimistic notion that when there is a crisis fate produces a man big enough to meet it.

The world finds it hard to speak of Mr. Wilson except in superlatives. A British journalist called him the other day, "the wickedest man in the world." This was something new in extravagance. I asked, "Why the wickedest?" He said, "Because he was so unable to forget himself that he brought the peace of the world down in a common smash with his own personal fortunes."

On the other hand General Jan Christian Smuts, writing with that perspective which distance gives, pronounces it to be not Wilson's fault but the fault of humanity that the vision of universal peace failed. Civilization was not advanced enough to make peace without vindictiveness possible.

This debate goes on and on. Mr. Wilson is either the worst hated or the most regretted personality of the Great War. The place of no one else is worth disputing. Lloyd George is the consummate politician, limited by the meanness of his art. Clemenceau is the personification of nationality, limited by the narrowness of his view. Mr. Wilson alone had his hour of superlative greatness when the whole earth listened to him and followed him; an hour which ended with him only dimly aware of his vision and furiously conscious of pin pricks.

You observe this inadequacy in Mr. Wilson, this incapacity to endure, at the outset of his career. It is characteristic of certain temperaments that when they first face life they should run away from it as Mr. Wilson did when, having studied law and having been admitted to the bar, he abandoned practice and went to teach in a girls' school. That was the early sign in him of that sense of unfitness for the more arduous contacts of life which was so conspicuous a trait during his presidency. He could not endure meeting men on an equal footing, where there was a conflict of wills, a rough clash of minds, where no concession was made to sensitiveness and egotism.

Some nervous insufficiency causes this shrinking, like the quick retreat from cold water of an inadequate body. Commonly a man who runs away from life after the first contact with it hates himself for his flight and there begins a conflict inside him which ends either in his admission of defeat and acknowledgment of his unfitness or in his convincing himself that his real motive was contempt of that on which he turned his back. If he admits to himself that he is really a little less courageous, a little more sensitive, a little less at home in this world, then he is gone. If he does satisfy himself that he is superior, has higher ideals, worthier ends, despises the ordinary arts of success he becomes arrogant, merely in self defense.

Mr. Wilson's "intellectual snobbism" was this kind of arrogance, acquired for moral self preservation, like that of the small boy who when his companions refuse to play with him says to himself that he is smarter than they are, gets higher marks in school, that he has a better gun than they have or that he, when he grows up, will be a great general while they are nobody. Almost everyone who feels himself unequal in some direction can satisfy himself that he exceeds in others. It is a common and human sort of arrogance, and Mr. Wilson had it inordinately.

He hated and contemned the law, in which life had given him his first glimpse of his frailty. He

28

would have no lawyers make the peace or draft the covenant of the league of nations. Lawyers were pitiful creatures,—he kept one of them near him, Mr. Lansing, admirably chosen, to remind him of how contemptible they were, living in fear of precedents, writing a barbarous jargon out of deeds and covenants, impeding the freedom of the imagination with their endless citations.

He despised politicians, he despised business men, he despised the whole range of men who pursue worldly arts with success. He despised the qualities which he had not himself, but like all men who are arrogant self protectively he was driven to introspection and analyzed himself pitilessly.

The public got glimpses of these analyses. Sometimes he called that something in him which left him less fit for the world than the average, a little regretfully, "his singletrack mind." Sometimes it leaped to light as an object of pride, his arrogance again, a pride that was "too great to fight," like the common run of men,—in the law courts or on the battlefields. He kept asking himself the question, "Why am I not as other men are?", and sometimes his nature would rise up in protest and he would exclaim that he was as other

men were and would pathetically tell the world
that he was "misunderstood," that he was not
cold and reserved but warm and genial and kindly,
only largely because the world would see him as he
was.

But always the one safe recourse, the one assurance of personal stability was arrogance. Contempt was the most characteristic habit of his
mind. Out of office he is no sage looking charitably
at the fumbling of his successor.

A friend who has seen him since his retirement
describes him as watching "with supreme contempt" the executive efforts of Mr. Harding.
Washington gossip credits him with inventing the
phrase, "the bungalow mind," to describe the
present occupant of the White House. Another
remark of his about the new President is said to
have been "I look forward to the new administration with no unpleasant anticipations, except those
caused by Mr. Harding's literary style."

There is always his contrast of others with himself to their disadvantage, mentally or morally, as
writers, or leaders, or statesmen. So full a life as
Mr. Wilson led in the last dozen or more years
ought to have made him less self-conscious. A
robuster person would have hated with a certain

zest, continued with a certain gaiety, laughed as he fought, found something to respect in his foes, seen the curtain fall upon his own activities with a certain cheerfulness.

He seems deficient in resources. He had not that gusto which richly endowed natures ordinarily have. He found no fun in measuring his strength with other men's. There was a certain overstrain about him, which made him cushion himself about with non-resistant personalities. He lacked curiosity. His fine mind seemed to want the energy to interest itself in the details of any subject that filled it, and this was one of his fatal weaknesses at the Peace Conference. Perhaps it was a deficiency of vital force. Moreover he came to his great task tired. His life till he was past fifty was one of defeat. There was the early disappointment and turning back from law practice, the giving up of his youthful ambition for a public career to which he had trained himself passionately by the study of public speaking. Dr. Albert Shaw, who was his fellow student at Johns Hopkins, says that in the University Mr. Wilson was the finest speaker, except possibly the old President of the College, Dr. Daniel Cort Gilman.

Then there were the long years of poverty as a

college professor, when he overworked at writing and university extension lectures, to make his small salary as a teacher equal to the support of his family, his three children and his aged parents. There was his failure at literature, for his *History of the United States* brought him neither fame nor money, the public finding it dull and unreadable.

Then the crowning unsuccess as President of Princeton; for when his luck changed and a political career opened to him as Governor of New Jersey, with trustees and alumni against him, nothing seemed to be before him but resignation and a small professorship in a Southern College. It was a straightened life that he had led when he came to Washington for the first time as President, scandalizing the servants of the White House with the scantness of his personal effects. There had been neither the time nor the means nor probably the energy for larger human contacts. And something inherent always held him back from the world, something which diverted him to academic life, which when he was writing his *Congressional Government*, his best book, held him in Baltimore, almost a suburb of Washington, where he read what he wrote to his fellow-students at Johns Hopkins, whose livelier curiosity took them often to the galleries of the House and the Senate about which he was writing from a distance.

Those to whom life is kinder than it was during many years to Mr. Wilson have naturally a zest for it. Robuster natures than his even though life averts her face, often preserve a zest for it. Conscious of his powers he seems to have fortified himself against failure with scorn. He had a scorn for the intellects of those who succeed by arts which he did not possess. He had scorn for politicians. He had a scorn for wealth. He had a scorn for his enemies. He had a scorn for Republicans. He had a scorn for the men with whom he had to deal in Europe, the heads of the Allied Governments.

Above all he scorned Lloyd George, an instinct telling him that the British Premier had a thousand arts where he himself, unschooled in conference with equals, had none. He said of Lloyd George just before he sailed for Paris, suspecting him of treachery to the League of Nations, "I shall look him in the eye and say to him Damn you, if you do not accept the League I shall go to the people of Great Britain and say things to them that will shake your government."

When he made this threat he could not foresee that the compromise of the Peace would leave him with so little character that British Liberals, their faith destroyed, should in the end couple his name with their own Premier's and exclaim, "Your man Wilson talks like Jesus Christ, but he acts like Lloyd George!"

More than all others he scorned Lodge. The Massachusetts Senator who had put by scholarship for politics and had won the opportunity to do menial service for a political machine hated the man who had chosen scholarship, for whatever motive, and come out with the Presidency. You hate the man you might perhaps have been if you had chosen more boldly, more according to your heart—if you are like Mr. Lodge.

A life of demeaning himself to politicians, of waiting for dead men's shoes in the Senate, had, however, brought some compensations to Lodge, among others an inordinate capacity to hurt. The Massachusetts Senator could get under the President's skin as no other man could. Washington is a place where every whisper is heard in the White House.

Mr. Lodge's favorite private charge uttered in a tone of withering scorn was that the President failed to respond as a man would to the national insult offered by Germany in sinking the Lusitania

34

because there was something womanish about him
and he would tell, to prove it, how Wilson went
white and almost collapsed over the news that
blood had been shed through the landing of
American marines at Vera Cruz.

The President hardly failed to hear this. Perhaps it reminded him of that something in him
which he was always trying to forget, that something which diverted his life toward failure at the
outset, which once betrayed him, with a strange
mixture of the arrogance and inferiority, into his
famous words "too proud to fight."

At any rate mutual comprehension and hatred
between these two men was instinctive, each having the opposite choice in the beginning and neither
in his heart perhaps ever having forgiven himself
wholly for his choice. Mr. Wilson could never get
Mr. Lodge wholly out of his mind in the last two
years of his Presidency, a disability which pre-
vented him from looking quite calmly and sanely
at public questions.

The story of the President's appeal for a Democratic Congress in 1918 which has never been fully
told, illustrates the bearing this Lodge obsession
had upon Mr. Wilson's later fate. When the Congressional election was approaching ex-Congress-

man Scott Ferris, then acting as Chairman of the
Democratic National Committee, went to the
President and told him that there was danger of
losing both houses of Congress, the lower house not
being important, but the Senate as a factor in
foreign relations, Mr. Ferris suggested, was indispensable to the Democratic party. Mr. Wilson
was more hopeful but agreed to take under advise-
ment some sort of appeal to the country. It was
not desired that this should be anything more than
a letter, perhaps to Mr. Ferris, intended for pub-
lication, and pointing out the need of support for
the President's policies in the next Congress.

Shortly afterward Mr. Tumulty, the President's
Secretary, brought to the Shoreham Hotel in Washington an appeal to the country for a Democratic
Congress and read it to several Democrats gathered
there for the purpose, including Homer S. Cummings, who, by that time, had become acting
Chairman of the Democratic National Committee
and was in charge of the campaign. Mr. Cummings doubted the wisdom of an appeal, couched
in such terms as the one Mr. Tumulty read. He
took it to Vance McCormick, Chairman of the
Democratic National Committee, who, because he
was Chairman of the War Trade Board, was not

taking part in the election. Mr. McCormick agreed
with Mr. Cummings that the appeal as written
would do more harm than good to the Democratic
party, saying that the war had not been conducted
on a partisan basis, that some of his own associates
on the War Trade Board were Republicans and
that Mr. Wilson should ask for the reëlection of all
who had been loyal supporters of the war, whether
Republicans or Democrats.

The appeal to the country as it then stood contained a bitter denunciation of Senator Lodge.
What Wilson chiefly saw in a Republican victory
was himself at the mercy of the man he hated worst,
the Massachusetts Senator. Mr. McCormick
thought that if the President was going to name
names he must, at least, denounce Claude Kitchen,
the Democratic leader of the House, as well as
Senator Lodge. If Mr. Wilson would ask for the
reëlection of those who had been loyal, of whatever party, listing the offenders, of both parties,
including Mr. Lodge if he must, Mr. McCormick
believed that the impression on the country would
be favorable and thus a Democratic Congress
might be elected.

Being agreed, Mr. Cummings and Mr. McCormick went to the White House and argued for a

less partisan appeal. All they accomplished was the striking of Mr. Lodge's name out of the appeal by convincing Mr. Wilson that he could not attack the Republican Senator while ignoring the worse offenses of Mr. Kitchen and Champ Clark in his own party.

For the rest, the President made the appeal more purely personal and more partisan than before. He could not get the Lodge obsession out of his mind. He could not bring himself to ask for the election of members of Mr. Lodge's party. The wisdom of Mr. Cummings and Mr. McCormick was soon vindicated. The appeal with Mr. Lodge's name out was only a shade less impolitic than it would have been with his name in. It gave Mr. Lodge his majority in the Senate and turned the peace into a personal issue between the two "scholars in politics."

By this time Mr. Wilson had lost his sense of actuality. He could ask the nation for a Congress to his liking as a personal due. He could condemn Mr. Lodge as an enemy of those purposes with which we entered the war, simply because Mr. Lodge could hurt him as no other man could. The President had been talking for some months to the whole world and the whole world had listened with

profound attention. His mission had taken, unconsciously perhaps, a Messianic character. His
enemies were the enemies of God. The ordinary
metes and bounds of personality had broken down.
The state of mind revealed in the appeal as originally written was the state of mind of the Peace
Conference and of the fight over the Treaty and
the League which succeeded the Peace Conference.
All that happened afterwards, including the pitiful
personal tragedy, had become inevitable.

For a while at Paris amid the triumphs of his
European reception and the successes of the first
few months up to the adoption of the League
covenant Mr. Wilson forgot Mr. Lodge, forgot him
too completely.

It was my fortune to see him at the apex of his
career. He was about to sail for America on that
visit which he made here in the midst of the treaty
making. His League covenant had just been
agreed to. The world had accepted him. Fate
had led him far from those paths of defeat and obscurity into which his sensitiveness and shyness
had turned him as a youth. He was elated and
confident. He looked marvelously fresh and young,
his color warm and youthful, his eye alive with
pleasure.

He talked long and well, answered questions freely, told stories of his associates at the peace table, especially of one who never read the memoranda his secretaries prepared, who was so deaf that he could not hear a word spoken in conference and who spoke so loudly that no one could interrupt him. "What could one do," Mr. Wilson asked, "to penetrate a mind like that?" M. Clemenceau, who unlike this other commissioner, had eyes and saw not, had ears and neither would he hear, had said to him once, in response to a firm negative, "You have a heart of steel!" "I felt like replying to him," flashed Mr. Wilson, "I have not the heart to steal!"

So well poised, so sure of himself he felt that he could do an extraordinary thing. He could laugh off a mistake. Robuster natures accept mistakes as a child accepts tumbles. Mistakes for Mr. Wilson were ordinarily crises for his arrogancy.

You may judge, then, how confident he was at that supreme moment. He could brush aside a great mistake lightly. Someone asked him, "What about the freedom of the seas?"

"The freedom of the seas!" he answered, "I must tell you about that. It's a great joke on me. I left America thinking the freedom of the seas the most important issue of the Peace Conference. When I got here I found there was no such issue. You see the freedom of the seas concerns neutrals in time of war. But when we have the League of Nations there will be no neutrals in time of war. So, of course, there will be no question of the freedom of the seas. I hadn't thought the thing out clearly."

From that moment the decline began. Mr. Wilson had unwisely chosen to have his victory first and his defeats afterward, always bad generalship.

Compromise followed compromise, each one destructive. The fourteen points were impaired until Mr. Wilson hated to be reminded of them by Lloyd George, in the case of Dantzig and the Polish corridor. The dawn of a better world grew dubious. The ardor of mankind cooled. They were at first incredulous, then skeptical.

The President saw only slowly the consequences of that chaffering to which Mr. Lloyd George and M. Clemenceau led him. He was a poor merchant. He dealt in morals and could cast up no daily balance. He was busy with details for which his mind had no sufficient curiosity or energy. Mr. Keynes, in his remarkable description of Mr.

Wilson making peace, says that his mind was slow.

Doubtless it was slow in political trading about the council table, just as a philosopher may be slow in the small talk of a five o'clock tea.

Mr. Wilson was out of his element in the conference; Mr. Lloyd George and M. Clemenceau were in theirs. Gradually the conviction entered Mr. Wilson's soul that what was being destroyed at Paris was Mr. Wilson. The figure of Senator Lodge began to rise across the Atlantic, malevolent and evil, the Lodge against whom he had wanted to appeal to the American people.

The strain was telling upon him. He had to sit beside his destroyers with that smiling amiability which Mr. Lansing records in his book. He had to deal with men on a basis of equality, a thing which he had run away from doing in his youth, which all his life had made too great demands upon his sensitive, arrogant nature.

One whose duty it was to see him every night after the meetings of the Big Three reports that he found him with the left side of his face twitching. To collect his memory he would pass his hand several times wearily over his brow. The arduousness of the labor was not great enough to account for this. M. Clemenceau at nearly eighty

stood the strain and an assassin's bullet as well.
Mr. Lloyd George thrived on what he did. But
the issue was not personal with them. Neither
was assisting, with difficult amiability, at his own
destruction. The time came when he might have
had back some of the ground he had given. Mr.
Lloyd George offered it to him. He would not
have it. What it was proposed to amend was not
so much the peace treaty as Mr. Wilson himself,
and he could not admit that he needed amendment.

The issue had become personal and Mr. Lodge,
upon Mr. Wilson's return, with malevolent understanding, kept it personal. The Republicans made
their fight in the one way that made yielding by
the President impossible. They made it nominally
on the League but really on Mr. Wilson. The
President might have compromised on the League,
but he could not compromise on Mr. Wilson. Of
such involvement in self there could be only one
end.

Like a poet of one poem, Mr. Wilson is a statesman of one vision, an inspiring vision, but one
which his own weakness kept him from realizing.
His domestic achievements are not remarkable,
his administration being one in which movements
came to a head rather than one in which much was

initiated. He might have cut the war short by two years and saved the world much havoc, if he had begun to fight when the *Lusitania* was sunk. Once in the war he saw his country small and himself large; he did not conceive of the nation as winning the war by sending millions of men to France; he saw himself as winning the war by talking across the Atlantic. At the Peace Conference he did not conceive of his country's winning the peace by the powerful position in which victory had left it; he saw himself as winning the peace by the hold he personally had upon the peoples of Europe. Like Napoleon, of whom Marshal Foch wrote recently, "Il oublia qu'un homme ne peut etre Dieu; qu'au-dessus de l' individu, il y a la nation," he forgot that man can not be God; that over and above the individual there is the nation.

In politics he knew at first better than any other, again to quote Foch, that "above men is morality." This knowledge brought him many victories. But at critical junctures, as in his 1918 appeal to the voters and in the treaty fight, he forgot that morality was above one man, himself. He excelled in appeals to the heart and conscience of the nation, a gift Mr. Harding has not; the lesser arts

44

of the politician, tact and skill in the handling and selecting of men, were lacking.

He forgot in his greatness and aloofness the national passion for equality; which a more brilliant politician, Mr. Roosevelt, appeased by acting as the people's court jester, and which a shrewder politician, Mr. Harding, guards against by reminding the country that he is "just folks"; and in the end the masses turned upon him, like a Roman mob on a defeated gladiator.

GEORGE HARVEY

GEORGE HARVEY

THERE is something inscrutably ludicrous in the anxiety, bordering upon consternation, that lurks in the elongated and grotesque shadow that George Harvey casts upon Washington. The Republican fathers, who now feel a sense of responsibility, after a lapse of many years, for the future of party and country, do not yet know how to take him.

As a campaign asset his value could be expressed in intelligible terms. But as a party liability, or asset,—many a good Republican wishes he knew which,—he remains an enigma. There is not one of the array of elders of either political persuasion who, while laughing at his satirical sword-play, does not watch him covertly out of the corner of the eye, trembling at the potential ruin they consider him capable of accomplishing.

With all his weaknesses,—principally an almost hilarious political irregularity,—but two Republican hands were raised against him in the Senate when he was nominated for the Court of Saint James. When he rather unbecomingly filliped John Bull on the nose in his maiden speech as the premier ambassador, incidentally ridiculing some of his own countrymen's war ideals, President Harding and Secretary Hughes, gravely and with rather obvious emphasis, tried to set the matter aright as best they could. But there was no hint of reprimand; only a fervent hope that the mercurial Harvey would remain quiescent until the memory of the episode passed.

The quondam editor, now the representative of his country on the Supreme Council, in which capacity he is even more important than as Ambassador, represents a new strain in American politics. His mental habits bewilder the President, shock the proper and somewhat conventional Secretary of State, and throw such repositories of national divinity as Senators Lodge and Knox into utter confusion.

Harvey plays the game of politics according to his own rules, the underlying principle of which is audacity. He knows very well that the weak spot in the armor of nearly all politicians of the old school is their assumption of superiority, a sort of mask of benignant political venerability. They dread satire. They shrink from ridicule. A well-directed critical outburst freezes them. Such has been the Harvey method of approach. Having reduced his subjects to a state of terror, he flatters them, cajoles them, and finally makes terms with them; but he always remains a more or less unstable and uncertain quantity, potentially explosive.

There is not much of the present Harvey to be gleaned from his earlier experiences, except the pertinacity that has had much to do with his irregular climb up the ladder. He was born in Peacham, Vermont, where as a boy after school hours he mounted a stool in his father's general store and kept books. At the end of the year his accounts were short a penny. Because of this he received no Christmas gift not, as he has said, because his father begrudged the copper more than any other Vermont storekeeper, but because he was meticulously careful himself and expected the younger generation to be likewise.

This experience must have been etched upon Harvey's memory; no one can be more meticulous when his interest is aroused. To money he is indifferent, but a misplaced word makes him shudder. Writing with him is an exhausting process, which probably accounts for the fact that his literary output has been small. But the same power of analysis and attention to detail have been most effective in his political activities. In these his divination has been prophetic and in his manipulation of contending elements he shows a dexterity that has baffled even the professional politicians.

Harvey began his journalistic career upon the Peacham *Patriot*. Thence, with a borrowed ten dollar bill, he went to Springfield, serving his apprenticeship on the *Republican*, the best school of journalism in the country at that time. Later, on the Chicago *Evening News*, on the staff of which were Victor Lawson, Eugene Field, and Melville Stone, he completed his training.

When he joined the staff of the New York *World* at the age of twenty-one he was a competent, if not a brilliant newspaper man. His first important billet was the New Jersey editorship. This assignment across the river might very easily have been the first step toward a journalistic sepulcher, but not for Harvey. He made use of the post to garner an experience and knowledge of New Jersey politics that were to have an important bearing upon the career of Woodrow Wilson later. At the same time he attracted the attention of Joseph

Pulitzer who appointed him managing editor of the *World* before he was thirty.

While directing the *World's* policy during the second Cleveland campaign, Harvey met Thomas F. Ryan and William C. Whitney, the financial backers of the Democratic party. This prepared the way for his step from Park Row to Wall Street after his break with Pulitzer.

But the ways of Wall Street were not for Harvey. Nevertheless he was cautious enough to help himself to some of the profits that were forthcoming in those days of great amalgamations. With commendable foresight, however much he might have despised the methods then prevalent in the fields of high finance, he acquired enough to make him independent, to follow his own bent, and strangely enough, in the acquiring he came to the conclusion that the Republic could not survive if the plundering of the people by the "interests" continued as it was proceeding at that time.

He withdrew from the Street and eventually purchased *The North American Review*. In the meantime J. P. Morgan and Company had underwritten the bonds of the Harper publishing house and the elder Morgan asked Harvey to take charge of the institution. This he agreed to do with the understanding that he should be permitted to direct the policy of Harper's *Weekly*, one of the assets of the firm, without interference from the bankers.

With his peculiar faculty for detecting the weaknesses of financiers and politicians, Harvey now had before him an opportunity which was not afforded by the sedate old *North American Review* and he promptly took advantage of it. He had seen enough of the union of finance and politics to place little faith in either of the old parties. One was corrupt and powerful; the other was weak and parasitical. In both organizations money was a compelling consideration. Not being accustomed to think in terms of party allegiance Harvey decided that the only remedy for a very bad situation was a militant Democracy. He had the organ; next he needed the leader.

About this time, quite accidentally, he was present at Woodrow Wilson's inauguration as president of Princeton University. The professor appealed to the editor,—why, one can only conjecture. Perhaps it was a common abhorrence of machine politics, a passion for phrase turning, for there is a similarity in the methods of the two which separates them from the rank and file of ordinary

54

politicians. Harvey scrutinized Wilson more carefully, making a political diagnosis by a careful
examination of his works, and decided that he was
the man to turn the trick.

But the gap between the presidency of Princeton
and the Presidency of the United States was too
wide to be taken at one leap. Harvey concluded
that the governorship of New Jersey must be the
intermediate step. The Democratic year of 1910
provided the opportunity.

The New Jersey politicians did not care about
the college professor. They had already chosen a
candidate, but Harvey induced them to change
their minds. How this was accomplished is an
absorbing political tale, too long to be narrated
here. The New Jersey political leaders of that
period will tell you that if Mr. Wilson's "forward-
looking" men had controlled the convention he
never would have been nominated. They will also
tell you how Joseph Patrick Tumulty opposed the
nomination. They will even whisper that the con-
tests were settled rather rapidly that memorable
evening. After the nomination was announced,
Mr. Wilson's managers escorted him to the convention hall where he addressed a group of delegates
who were none too enthusiastic.

As they motored back to the hotel Mr. Wilson is reported to have asked: "By the way, gentleman, what was my majority?"

To which Mr. Nugent replied cryptically: "It was enough."

The question, at least in the presence of these gentlemen, it is said was never asked again.

Much has been said about the break between Mr. Harvey and Mr. Wilson. The published correspondence gives a fairly accurate picture of what happened at the Manhattan Club on the morning of the parting. I do not believe that Mr. Wilson dropped Colonel Harvey because he feared he was under Wall Street influence. The Harvey version sounds more plausible. According to this the erstwhile university professor had learned the technique of political strategy. He no longer felt that he was in need of guidance.

"I was not surprised at the excuse he gave a little later when the break came," said Harvey. "I would not have been surprised at any excuse he offered."

Mr. Harvey retired from the campaign. Harper's *Weekly* had been wrecked, whether or not by the espousal of the Wilson cause, and he sold it to Norman Hapgood who buried it in due course.

George Harvey might or might not have had visions of an appointment to the Court of St. James at that time. It is at least certain that his disappointment was keen, taking a form of vindictiveness which will survive as a distinct blot upon his career. In the preconvention campaign he aligned himself with the Champ Clark forces, but it was too late to undo the work he had done.

This episode is necessary to an understanding of what happened later. His transfer from the Democratic to the Republican party was a characteristically bold move. How genuine his later allegiance may be is a question which more than one Republican would like to have answered, but there is no doubt of the success of his coup. He is, at least where he wanted to be, occupying the post which he considers, in point of importance, next to the presidency itself, Mr. Hughes notwithstanding.

When the United States entered the war Harvey found himself in the secluded position of editor of the *North American Review*. This did not suit his disposition at all and he was very unhappy. He was too old to fight and it was not likely that he would be invited to Washington. In the meantime stories of mismanagement in the conduct of the war began to trickle out of the capital in devious undercurrents. The press, in a passive spirit of patriotism, was silent. Here was the opportunity.

In January, 1918, the first edition of the *North American Review War Weekly* appeared. Its editor announced that its purpose was to help win the war by telling the truth, the whole truth, and nothing but the truth. He defied the Creels, the Daniels, and the Burlesons, adopting the motto, "To hell with the censors and bureaucrats."

The journal was an instant success. Not only was it read with avidity but the Washington politicians were flabbergasted at the audacity of a man who dared to print what the press associations and the dailies would not touch. I do not think there can be any doubt of the genuineness of Harvey's motives at this time. His journal was rigidly nonpartisan. He spared no one whom he considered as an encumbrance in the winning of the war.

The most striking evidence of his attitude toward the Republican party at this time is found in the edition of the *Weekly* of March 9, 1918. Will H. Hays had just been elected chairman of the Republican National Committee. He made a speech extolling the virtues of his party. Of this Harvey made a stinging analysis denouncing Hays for invoking partisan spirit at so perilous an hour, concluding with this paragraph:

"As for Mr. Hays, with his insufferable claptrap about absolute unity as a blanket under which to gather votes while the very existence of the nation is threatened more ominously than anybody west of the Alleghanies—or in Washington, for that matter,—seems to realize, the sooner he goes home and takes his damned old party with him, the better it will be for all creation."

Surely no uncertain language! One might have supposed that the Chairman of the Republican Committee would have done nothing of the kind, but he did. Again the Harvey method was effective. Hays instead of resenting the denunciation wrote Harvey a rather abject letter, expressing the fear that he might have made a mistake in discussing politics during the war and asked for an interview.

Here another Harvey characteristic came into play. He did not assume the lofty role of mentor or prophet; he very tactfully and gently tucked the young Indianian under his wing. Thenceforth there were no more oratorical blunders.

Mr. Hays began to exhibit some capacity for

leadership; his speeches improved. From that day until the election of 1920 he never made one without George Harvey's counsel and approval.

This is as typical of Harvey as his audacity. He has a gentleness and charm quite unexpected in so savage a commentator. He will discuss and advise but he will not argue; and all of the time he will probe with uncanny accuracy for the weaknesses of those with whom he is dealing. It is rather by the weaknesses of others than by his own strength that he triumphs.

Eight months after his meeting with Hays, Harvey came to Washington where his shadow was cast over the destinies of the Republican party, which at that time consisted of a dozen elements with little in common except a hatred of Woodrow Wilson.

It was an ideal situation for the exercise of Harvey's peculiar talents. He met various factional leaders and before many weeks his house became their rendezvous, the G. H. Q. of the forces who were to encompass the defeat of Wilson. Harvey flattered and cajoled and counselled, enjoying himself immensely all of the time. This diversion was much more to his liking than the academic dignity of the editorship of the *North American Review*.

When President Wilson sailed away on his disastrous mission to Paris, Harvey's *Weekly* threw aside all restraint. It cut and slashed indiscriminately the President's policies. For the first time Harvey took on the guise of a Republican among Republicans. He even aided and abetted, with amused cynicism, the groping and fumbling of Republican leaders who were dazzled at the sudden break in the political clouds which had so long enshrouded them. He helped raise the funds used to counteract the league propaganda and toured the country in opposition to it.

The next shift in scenes was as much beyond Mr. Harvey's power of manipulation as it was beyond most of the Republicans who now sagaciously give the impression that their hands were on the ropes. Stories have been told of the great part Mr. Harvey played in the nomination of Mr. Harding. Mr. Harvey did not go to Chicago with the intention of supporting Mr. Harding any more than any other of the candidates, except Wood and Hiram Johnson, whom he despised.

He and the Senate oligarchy that coyly took the credit for nominating Mr. Harding turned to him when it was manifest that the machinery was stalled. Mr. Harding owes his nomination to a mob of bewildered delegates. It was not due to a wisely conceived nor brilliantly executed plan.

I doubt very much that George Harvey and President Harding had much in common until Harvey was invited to Marion. At that time the "irreconcilables" were beginning to be afraid that Elihu Root and William H. Taft were about to induce Mr. Harding to accept a compromise on the League of Nations. Harvey served the purpose of restoring the equilibrium. At the same time it is quite probable that the President was impressed by a mind so much more agile than his own. It was reasonably certain that it would not be diverted or misled by the intricacies of European diplomacy. And there was never any doubt of Harvey's Americanism.

The President's selection of Mr. Harvey for the London post is, of course, accounted for in other ways. There are some persons who profess to believe that Mr. Harding preferred to have the militant editor in London and his *Weekly* in the grave rather than to have him as a censor of Washington activities under the new régime. It can be said definitely that a sigh of relief went up from many a Republican bosom when the sacrilegious journal was brought to a timely end. And this did not happen, it is to be observed, until the nomination of George Harvey to the Court of St. James was duly ratified and approved by the Senate of the United States.

But if the *Weekly* has passed, the Republicans are still acutely conscious that Mr. Harvey is alive,—has he not reminded them of it in his first ambassadorial utterances?—and the journal is not beyond resuscitation. That is why Washington does not know whether to be chagrined or angry, whether to disavow or to condone. The discomfited Republicans frankly do not know what to think of it and probably will not so long as the amazing ambassador makes his own rules.

CHARLES EVANS HUGHES

CHARLES EVANS HUGHES

"Mais résiste-t-on a' la vertu? Les gens qui n'eurent point de faiblesses sont terribles," observed Sylvestre Bonnard of the redoubtable Therese.

This fearsomeness of the good is an old story. Horace remarked it, when, walking about near Rome, pure of heart and free from sin, he met a wolf. The beast quailed before his virtue and ran away,—to bark at the statue of the she wolf giving suck to Romulus, by way of intelligent protest.

A similar prevalence of virtue and a similar romantic quality, where it is least to be expected, was disclosed in a recent encounter between Charles Evans Hughes, Secretary of State, and one of the irreconcilables, when Mr. Hughes, *integer vitæ scelerisque purus* had just commissioned Colonel George Harvey to take the seat once occupied by Woodrow Wilson in the Supreme Council.

When the news of this appointment reached the

Capitol, Senator Brandegee, of Connecticut, hurried down to that structure across the street from the White House whose architectural style so markedly resembles the literary style of President Harding, the State War and Navy Building, official residence of Mr. Hughes.

Harvey being, in a sort, Brandegee's ambassador to the Court of Saint James, the Senator's object was to tell Mr. Hughes what Harvey should do in the Supreme Council. Mr. Brandegee has the gift of direct and forceful speech. In his earnestness, he dispenses with the elegancies and amenities. The upper ranges of his voice are not conciliatory.

In this tone, he developed views regarding this country's foreign relations with which Mr. Hughes could not agree. The Secretary of State combatted the Senator from Connecticut precisely as he combats counsel of the other side when a $500,000 fee is at stake. The discussion was energetic and divergent.

Mr. Brandegee hurried back to the Capitol and summoned other senators to his office, all those who were especially concerned about the exposure of Colonel Harvey to European entanglements.

He was excited. His voice was nasal. His language, in that select gathering, did not have to be parliamentary. He told the senators that they could expect the Versailles treaty by the next White House messenger; that "that whiskered,"—but nothing lies like direct quotes,—that "that whiskered" Secretary of State would soon get us into the League of Nations, being able for his purposes to wind President Harding about his little finger!

His excitement in such an emergency naturally communicated itself to his hearers. What to do? It was unanimously decided that the only adequate course was for Senator Henry Cabot Lodge to resign as Chairman of the Senate Foreign Relations Committee, by way of protest.

Henry Cabot Lodge running away from his chairmanship would be Henry Cabot Lodge behaving as romantically as Horace's wolf. The good are terrible, as Anatole France said in the words with which this sketch begins. It is not so much that you can not resist them, as that they lead you to make such fools of yourselves.

Mr. Hughes prevails, however, not merely by his virtue, but by his intelligence. His is the best mind in Washington; to this everyone agrees, and it is not excessive praise, for minds are not common in the Government.

Mr. Harding has not a remarkable one, the

people having decided by seven million majority
that it was best not to have one in the White House,
choosing instead, a good heart, excellent intentions,
and reasonable common sense. Mr. Hoover has a
fine business instinct, great but diffused mental
energy, but hardly an organized mind. From this
point the Cabinet grades down to the Secretary of
Labor, who, when Samuel Gompers, Jr., his Chief
Clerk, addressed him before visitors as, "Mr.
Secretary," said, "Please don't call me, 'Mr.
Secretary,' Sam. Call me, 'Jim.' I'm more used
to it."

"Call me Jim" is the mental sea level of the
Administration, by which altitudes are measured,
so let us not exalt Mr. Hughes' mind unduly, but
merely indicate what its habits are. Its operations
were described to me by a member of the Cabinet,
who said that no matter what subject was up for
discussion at a Cabinet meeting, it was always the
Secretary of State who said the final convincing
word about it, summing it all up, saying what
everyone else had been trying to say but no one
else had entirely succeeded in saying, simplifying
it, and all with an air of service, not of self-assertion.

Mr. Harding, speaking to an intimate friend,

said he had "two strong advisers,—Hughes and Hoover."

It is a satisfaction, even though it is not a delight, to come in contact with a mind like Mr. Hughes'; it is so definite, so hard and firm and palpable. You feel sure that it rests somewhere on the eternal verities. It is never agnostic. It has none of the morlaise of the twentieth century. Mr. Justice Brandeis, when Mr. Hughes was governor of New York and a reformer and progressive, said of him, "His is the most enlightened mind of the eighteenth century."

I think the Justice put it a century or two too late, for by the eighteenth century skepticism had begun to undermine those firm foundations of belief which Mr. Hughes still possesses. For him a straight line is the shortest distance between two points,—Einstein to the contrary, notwithstanding.

Conclusions rest upon the absolute rock of principle, as morality for his preacher father rested upon the absolute rock of the Ten Commandments. There is no doubt, no uncertainty, no nuance, no on the one hand, on the other, no discursiveness, no yielding to the seductions of fancy, but a stern keeping of the faith of the syllogism; a thing is so or it is not so. Mr. Hughes never hesitates. He never says, "I must think about that." He has thought about it. Or he turns instantly to his Principle and has the answer.

You speak of Mr. Hughes to ten men in the Capitol, and nine of them will say to you, "Of course it is easy to understand; his is the one real mind in Washington."

Everyone is impressed, for, starting with no other initiation into the mysteries of foreign relations than having had a father born in Wales and having spent his vacations in England, probably in the lake region studying the topography of Words-worth's poetry,—a certain oft detected resemblance to Wilson must make Wordsworth his favorite poet, as he was Wilson's,—in ten days was he not a great Secretary of State; and in three months the greatest Secretary of State? To be sure, back of him was the strongest nation on the earth, left so by the war, the one nation with resources, the ·creditor of all the others, to which a successful foreign policy would be naturally easy if it could only decide what that policy should be.

It was left to Mr. Hughes to say what it should be. His discovery of the word "interests," amazed Washington; it was so obvious, so simple that no one else had thought of it. Mr. Hughes' mind works like that;—hard, cold, unemotional, not to be turned aside, it simplifies everything, whether it be a treaty fight that has confused everyone else in the land, or a rambling Cabinet discussion; whether it be the mess in which the war left Europe, or the chaos in which watchful waiting left Mexico. His is a mind that delights in formulæ. He has one for Europe. He has one for Mexico. It is an analytical, not a synthetical mind, a lawyer's mind, not a creator's, like Wilson's, with, perhaps it may turn out, a fatal habit of over-simplification. Life is not a simple thing after all.

But effective simplification is instantly over-whelming; and he made his brief announcement, a few days after taking office, that the United States had won certain things as a belligerent, that it had not got them, that he was going after them, that other countries could expect nothing from us until they had recognized our rights and our in-terests; he had completely routed the Senate, which had been opposing Wilson's ideals with certain ideals of its own, pitting Washington's farewell address against "breaking the heart of the world," in a mussy statement of sentimentality.

Mr. Hughes talked of islands and oil and dollars; and the country came to its senses. Mr. Wilson

73

had pictured us going into world affairs as an international benefactor; it was sobby and suggested a strain on our pocketbooks. The Senate had pictured us staying out of them because our fathers had warned us to stay out and because the international confidence men would cheat us; it was Sunday-school-booky and unflattering. Mr. Hughes said we should go in to the extent of obtaining what was ours, and that we should stay out to the extent of keeping the others from obtaining what certainly was not theirs. It sounded grown-up; as a Nation we belonged not to the sob-sisterhood, neither were we tied to the apronstring of the Mothers of the Constitution.

Our national self-respect was restored. Truly, it required a mind to discover "interests" in the cloud of words that Mr. Wilson and the Senate had raised. Of course, it is all clear now, when everybody scorns idealism and talks glibly of interests. "Hobbs hints blue, straight he turtle eats; Nobbs prints blue, claret crowns his cup." But it was Hughes who "fished the murex up," who pulled "interests" out of the deep blue sea of verbal fuddlement.

And thinking of our dollars, thanks to Mr. Hughes, we are made sane and whole, clearsighted and unafraid, standing erect among the nations of the earth asking lustily for Yap.

Our foreign relations had been the subject of passion. Mr. Hughes made them the subject of reason. Mr. Wilson could think of nothing but his hatred of Lodge, which rendered an agreement with the Senate impossible, and his hatred of Lloyd George and Marshal Foch, which rendered coöperation with the Allies and through it achievements in the foreign field that would have reconciled the public to his policies, equally impossible.

Mr. Hughes looked at his task objectively. He saw the power of the United States. He saw how easy it was to exert that power diplomatically. He saw the simple and immediate concerns of the United States. Foch says that he won the war, "by smoking his pipe," meaning by keeping cool and regarding his means and ends with the same detachment with which he would study an old campaign of Napoleon. I do not know on what sedative Mr. Hughes wins his diplomatic victories, as he does not smoke a pipe;—perhaps by reading the *Sunday School Times*. But like the French Marshal, he knows the secret of keeping his head. It is a great quality of mind not to lose it when you most need it. Mr. Hughes has it. Perhaps this is why Washington remarks his mind; he always has it with him.

"I am not thinking of myself in my work here," he said once. "I don't care about immediate acclaim. I am counsel for the people of this country. If a generation from now they think their interests have been well represented, that will be enough."

He is coldly objective.

Mr. Hughes comes by his coolness naturally. He was born to it, which is the surest way to come by anything. Men have hated him for it, coolness being a disconcerting quality, ever since he emerged from obscurity in New York during the insurance investigation, calling it his "coldness" and adding by way of good measure the further specification, his "selfishness."

If the last characterization is to stand, it should be amended to read, his "enlightened selfishness." He has a good eye for his own interests. Roosevelt disliked him for it, because when governor and again when candidate for president, he refused to gravitate into the Roosevelt solar system, taking up his orbit like the rest of them about the Colonel. But think what happened to that system when the great sun of it went out!

CHARLES EVANS HUGHES

His political associates in New York hated him, accused him of being "for nothing but Hughes," when he quit them in the fight "to hand the government back to the people" and went, on the invitation of President Taft, upon the Supreme Bench. But it was his only way out. If he had gone on working with them, he would still be "handing the government back to the people" along with,—but who were the great figures of 1910? He knows an expiring issue and its embarrassments by an unerring instinct. He finds a new one, such as "our national interests," with as sure a sense.

It is worth while casting a glance at him "smoking his pipe," when other real and false opportunities presented themselves to him; one finds discrimination. He refuses a Republican nomination for Mayor of New York City when there is not a chance of electing a Republican Mayor of New York City. He accepts a Republican nomination for Governor of New York State, when the putting up of Hearst as the Democratic candidate makes the election of a Republican as Governor of New York State morally certain. He refuses the Republican nomination for President, in 1912, when another, viewing himself and his party less objectively, through vanity perhaps, might have believed that his own nomination was the one thing needed to prevent that year's Republican cataclysm. Four years later he accepts the Republican nomination for President, when as the result showed, there is at least a reasonable chance to win. He takes the post of Secretary of State when neglected opportunities lie ready to his hand and when the force of world events requires little more than his intelligent acquiescence to bring him diplomatic success.

His discovery of "interests" was no accident. It sprang from that hard unemotional simplifying habit of his mind.

When one writes of Mr. Hughes, men ask, pardonably, "Which Mr. Hughes? The old Mr. Hughes, or the new Mr. Hughes?" for he has had, as the literary critics would say, his earlier and his later manner.

But it is chiefly manner, a smile recently achieved, a different way of wearing the beard, a little less of the stern moralist, a little more of the man of the world. A connoisseur of Hughes, who has studied him for nearly twenty years, after a recent observation, pronounced judgment: "It's the same Hughes, a trifle less cold, but just as dry." And the Secretary of State himself, when one of the weeklies contained an article on "The New Mr. Hughes," remarked, "People did not understand me then, that is all."

These two eminent authorities being substantially agreed for the first time during many divergent years, there must be something in it. Mr. Hughes must be a gradually emerging personality. You take that new warmth, recently detected; Mr. Hughes himself knows it was always there. It is like the light ray of a star which has needed a million years to reach the earth; it was always there but it required a long time to get across.

Then the beard:—when Mr. Hughes was "handing the government back to the people" in New York, it was a preacher's beard; you might have encountered its like anywhere among the circuit riders. Now it is a foreign secretary's beard; you might encounter it in any European capital,—a world statesman's beard. The change of beard reveals the smile, which was probably always there, and the splendid large teeth. The nose, standing out in bolder relief, is handsomer and more distinguished. You see more of Mr. Hughes than you used to and you gain by the improved vision.

Something has dropped from him, however, beside the ends of the whiskers. I met him first when he was about to run for President in 1916. An icy veil, like frozen mist, seemed to hang between us. We talked through it ineffectively. When I saw him again as Secretary of State, that chill barrier had fallen away; to recur to my figure, he gradually emerges.

Mr. Hughes of the later manner is, however, I am persuaded after long familiarity with his career, more truly Hughesian than the Hughes of the earlier manner; just as the Henry James of the later manner is more explicitly Jamesian than the James of the earlier manner, and the Cabot Lodge of the present is much more irretrievably Cabotian than the Cabot Lodge who years ago stood with reluctant feet where the twin paths of scholarship and politics meet,—and part.

I should say that Mr. Hughes was Bryan plus the advantages, which Mr. Bryan never enjoyed, of a correct Republican upbringing and a mind. The Republican upbringing and the mind have come of late years to preponderate. Looking at Mr. Hughes to-day, you could not tell him from a Republican, except perhaps by his mind, though such esoteric Republicans as Brandegee, Cabot Lodge, and Knox profess an ability to distinguish.

But when he was "handing the government back

to the people" in New York, there was too much Bryan about him. The Republicans would have none of him, except as a choice of evils,—the greater evil being defeat. They called him ribald names. They referred to him scornfully as "Wilson with whiskers," when they ran him, reluctantly, for the Presidency in 1916. His opponent being also of the Bryan school, and a minister's son at that, Hughes striving for an issue, failed to make it clear which was which, a doubt that remained until the last vote from California was finally counted after the election. This was the Mr. Hughes of the earlier manner.

Latterly, Mr. Hughes has succeeded in establishing the distinction which he did not succeed in making during that campaign. When he confronted the task of Secretary of State, he carefully studied the international career of Woodrow Wilson, as a sort of inverse Napoleon, a sort of diplomatic bad example.

"This," he said to himself, "was a mistake of Wilson," and he noted it. "And this," he observed thoughtfully, "was another mistake of Wilson. I shall avoid it." "This," he again impressed on his memory, "was where Lloyd George and Clemenceau trapped him. I shall keep out of that pit."

His head, like a book of etiquette, is full of "Don'ts," diplomatic "Don'ts," all deduced from the experience of Wilson.

The former President met Europe face to face. Mr. Hughes thanks his stars for the breadth of the Atlantic. The former President put his League of Nations first on his program. Mr. Hughes puts his League of Nations last, to be set up after every other question is settled.

The former President tried to sell the Country pure idealism. Now as a people we have the habit of wars in which we seek nothing, but after which, in spite of ourselves, a little territory, a few islands, or a region out of which we subsequently carve half a dozen States, is found adhering to us. Mr. Wilson offered us a war in which, of course, we sought nothing and found, at the end of it, not the customary few trifles of territory, but the whole embarrassing, beggarly world adhering to us. The thumbscrew and the rack could not wring from Mr. Hughes the admission that we are after anything more lofty than our interests.

One of the present Secretary's "Don'ts" of similar derivation is "Don't have a fight with the Senate unless you make sure first that you have the public with you."

Mr. Hughes does not run away from fights; he likes them. But believing God to be on the side with the most battalions, and intending scrupulously to observe this last "Don't," in order to secure the necessary popular support, he is as Secretary of State, "handing the government back to the people," just as he did when governor,—a little less self-consciously, perhaps, a little less noisily, but still none the less truly.

He is the most democratic Secretary of State this Country has ever had, and this includes Bryan to whose school, as has just been remarked, he originally belonged. If we are ever to have democratic control of foreign relations, it will be by the methods of Mr. Hughes, because of the training and beliefs of Mr. Hughes, and as a consequence of the most undemocratic control of foreign relations which our Constitution attempted to fasten upon us.

A successful foreign policy requires public understanding and support. The makers of the Constitution established in our government a nice balance of powers between the various departments, beautifully adjusted until someone thought of putting a stone into one side of the balance. That stone is the people. The Fathers of the Constitution had not noticed it. The executive put it into its end of the balance some years ago, and the legislative has been kicking the beam ever since. One nice bit of balancing was that between the Senate and the Executive on treaty making. In foreign relations, the President can do everything, and he can do nothing without the approval of two thirds of the Senate. It is a nice balance, which broke the heart of John Hay, frittered away the sentimentalities of Mr. Bryan, and destroyed Mr. Wilson.

No one ever thought of putting the stone into it until the Senate did so two years ago, by discussing the Versailles treaty in the open, right before the public. The people got into the scale, and Mr. Wilson hit the sky.

Mr. Hughes observed what happened. He is determined that the stone this time shall go in on his end of the balance. He talks to the country daily. He takes the people into his confidence, telling all that can be told and as soon as it can be told. He makes foreign relations hold front pages with the Stillman divorce case. He makes no step without carrying the country with him. He comes as near conducting a daily referendum on what we shall do for our "interests" as in a country so big as ours can be done; and that is democratic control of foreign relations, initiated by the Senate, for its own undoing.

Into that balance where he is placing the stone, he will put more of mankind's destinies than any other man on earth holds in his hands to-day. His has been a long way up from the shy, sensitive youth that one who knew him when he was beginning the law describes to me. He was then unimaginably awkward, incapable of unbending, a wet blanket socially. An immense effort of will has gone into fashioning the agreeable and habitual diner-out of to-day, into profiting by the mistakes of the New York governorship, of the campaign of 1916.

One sees still the traces of the early stiffness; the face is sensitive; the eyes drop, seldom meeting yours squarely; when they do, they are the mild eyes of the Church! I suppose the early experiences of the Church help him.

His attitude toward Colonel Harvey's and other of the President's diplomatic appointments takes its color from his good father's attitude toward the problem of evil. God put evil in the world, and it is not for man to question. The President sends the Harveys abroad; they are not Mr. Hughes', but his own personal representatives. It is not for Mr. Hughes to question.

He grows a better Republican every day. And the Republicans of the Senate are not reconciled. They feel like the man who saw the hippopotamus:

> If he should stay to tea, I thought,
> There won't be much for us.

There won't be much for them. Enthusiasm grows among them over his admirable fitness for reinterment on the Supreme Bench.

EDWARD MANDELL HOUSE

EDWARD M. HOUSE

THE nature of Colonel Edward M. House was fully revealed by a story of his youth, which he told me at Paris in the concluding moments of the Peace Conference. He was elated and confident. The compromises in which he delighted had been made. The gifts had all been bestowed—of territory which men will have to fight for to keep, of reparations which will never be paid, of alliances which will never be carried out, of a League of Nations which the Colonel's own Nation will never enter.

Looking the work over with that blindness with which men are struck who are under the dominion of another and stronger man's mind, his gentle soul was flooded with happiness. He was as near boasting as one of his modest habits could be, as his mind turned to the wisdom of his youth which had brought forth this excellent fruit.

"I got my first real sight of politics," he said,

"when I was a boy in Cornell University. My great chum there was young Morton, a son of the Democratic war governor of Indiana. The Hayes-Tilden contest over the Presidency was being decided. Morton and I used to run away from Ithaca to Washington during that absorbing fight. By reason of his father's position in the Democratic party, he could get in behind the scenes as few young men could; and he took me with him. I saw the whole amazing thing. I made up my mind then and there that only three or four men in this country counted, and that there was little chance of rising to be one of those three or four by the ordinary methods."

He was, when he said this, at the apex of his career, behind the scenes of the greatest World Congress ever held, following the greatest War the world had ever known. And he had been behind the scenes as had no other man, in Europe as a privileged onlooker with both belligerents, and in America as the confidant of tremendous events.

He was there, as in his college days, at the Hayes-Tilden contest, by grace of a friend whose influence had been sufficient to secure him his opportunities. The parallel was in his mind, and he regarded it with self-approval. He had chosen his course and chosen it wisely. It had led him to the greatest peace-making in history.

There was a little more self-revelation. He and Morton had prepared for college with Yale in view. But Morton had flunked his entrance examinations at Yale and afterward succeeded in passing the Cornell tests. House had gone to Cornell to be with his friend, an early indication of a capacity for self-effacement, for attachment to the nearest great man at hand who could take him behind the scenes.

The mystery of Colonel House is that he has been possessed all his life, almost passionately, with that instinct which makes boys run to fires. His fastening upon the favorably placed, whether it was Morton in his youth, or Wilson in his maturity, was not ordinary self-seeking, not having for its object riches or power or influence. It was merely desire to see for the pure love of seeing.

His is a boundless curiosity about both men and events. His eyes are the clue to his character. Boardman Robinson, with the caricaturist's gift for catching that feature which exhibits character, said to me one day during the War, "I just passed Colonel House on the street. The most wonderful seeing eyes I ever saw!"

Nature had made Colonel House all eyes—
trivial in figure, undistinguished, slightly ludicrous,
almost shambling, shrinking under observation so
that he gained a reputation for mystery, with only
one feature to catch your attention, a most amazingly fine pair of eyes. It was as if nature had
concentrated on those eyes, treating all the puny
rest of him with careless indifference. They are
eyes that delight in seeing, eyes to seek a place
in the first row of the grand stand of world events,
eyes that turn steadily outward upon objective
reality. Not the eyes of a visionary—House got
his visions of the brotherhood of man and the rest
of it at second-hand from Wilson—eyes that glow
not with the internal fires of a great soul, but with
the intoxication of the spectacle.

And with the eyes nature had given House an
unerring instinct for getting where, with his small
figure, he could see. The ego of the passionate
spectator is as peculiar as that of the book col-
lector or the curiosity hunter. Given a shoulder
tall enough the diminutive House perches upon
it, like a small boy watching a circus parade from
his father's broad back, whether the shoulder be
Morton's in his youth, or Wilson's in his maturity.

Some have tried to explain House by saying that

he had the vanity of loving familiarity with the great; but I doubt if House cared for kings, as kings, any more than a bibliomaniac cares for jade. He wanted to see; and kings were merely tall objects on which to perch and regard the spectacle.

He remained simple and unaffected by his contacts with Europe, did none of the vulgar aping of the toady, coming away from the Peace Conference an unconscious provincial, who said "Eyetalian" in the comic-paper way, and Fiume pronouncing the first syllable as if he were exclaiming "Fie! for shame!"—an unspoiled Texan who must have cared as little what kings and potentates thought of him as a newsboy watching a baseball game cares for the accidental company of a bank president.

The world has been good to Colonel House, according to his standards. He has realized his ambition to the fullest. Life has given him all he wanted, the privilege of seeing, more abundantly than to any other in his generation, perhaps in all time; for he is history's greatest spectator.

He is glad. His heart is full. He wishes to give in return. He is the kindest-hearted man who has ever had empires at his disposal. He wants to give, give, give. He wants to make happy. He was the fairy godmother of Europe, the diplomatic Carnegie, who thought it a disgrace to die diplomatically rich.

For many months I saw him almost daily at Paris. His was a heart of gold, whether in personal or international relations; but a heart of gold does not make a great negotiator. Perverse and nationalistic races of men, incredulous of the millenium, keep their hearts of gold at home when they go out to deal with their neighbors.

It was difficult for Colonel House to say no. He might go so far as to utter the first letter of that indispensable monosyllable; but before he accomplished the vowel, his mind would turn to some happy "formula" passing midway between no and yes. He was fertile in these expedients. Daily he would talk of some new "formula," for Fiume, for Dantzig, for the Saar Valley, for the occupation of the Rhine, for Shantung, always happily, always hopefully. The amiable William Allen White hit off his disposition perfectly when he said House's daily prayer was, "Give us this day our daily compromise."

When he split a hair between the south and southwest side, it was not for logistic pleasure; it was to divide it with splendid justice and send each of two rival claimants away happy in the possession of exactly half of the slender filament, so that neither would be empty handed. I never saw a man so overjoyed as he was one day late in April or early in May when M. Clemenceau had left his rooms in the Hotel Crillon with the promise of Franco-American defensive alliance.

"The old man," he said, "is very happy. He has got what he has been after. I can't tell you just now what it is. But he has got it at last."

He had been the donor, for Mr. Wilson, of the exact southwest side of a hair, the promise to submit, without recommendations, an alliance to the United States Senate, which had little prospect of ever being accepted by this country. The sight of the French Premier's happiness made him radiant.

It was not merely because representatives of foreign governments found Colonel House easy to see when they could not gain access to President Wilson that kept a throng running to his quarters in the Crillon; it was because there they found the line of least resistance. There was the readiest sympathy. There was the greatest desire to accommodate. He sought always for a formula that would satisfy the claims of all.

A man so ready to compromise is actuated by no guiding principle. Mr. Scott, the editor of the *Manchester Guardian*, said when President Wilson was in England; "Yes, Lloyd George is honestly for the League of Nations. But that won't prevent him from doing things at Paris which will be utterly inconsistent with the principle of such a league. It isn't intellectual dishonesty; but Lloyd George hasn't a logical mind. He doesn't understand the implications of his own position."

Neither did Colonel House at Paris. The League of Nations was an emotion with him, not a principle. It was a tremendous emotion. He spoke of it in a voice that almost broke. I remember his glowing eyes and the little catch in his throat as he said, at Paris, "The politicians don't like the League of Nations. And if they really knew what it would do to them, they would like it still less."

But, for all that naïve faith in the wonders it would do, Colonel House had not thought out the League of Nations, and was quite incapable of thinking it out, for he is not a man of analytical mind; and what mental power he had was inhibited by the glow of his feelings. His temperature was above the thinking point. Thus, like Mr. Lloyd

George, he could make compromises that played ducks and drakes with his general position, since he had no real understanding of the League, which was not an intellectual conviction with him, arduously arrived at, but which possessed his soul as by an act of grace, like an old-fashioned religious conversion.

He was loyal at heart to Mr. Wilson and to everything that was Mr. Wilson's, his mind being absorbed into Mr. Wilson's, and having no independent existence. There are natures which demand an utter and unquestioning loyalty in those to whom they yield their confidence, and Mr. Wilson's was of that sort, as a remark of his about Secretary Colby will indicate.

When Mr. Lansing was removed from office, the country was astounded to learn that he was to be succeeded by Bainbridge Colby. The President communicated his decision first to one of the few who then had access to his sick room. This adviser ventured to expostulate.

"Mr. Colby," he said, "is brilliant, but he is uncertain. His whole career has lacked stability. He is not known to have the qualities which the Nation has been taught to expect in a Secretary of State."

"At any rate," replied the President sharply, "he is loyal."

At any rate, Colonel House was loyal.

The ego of Mr. Wilson demanded and received utter loyalty from him, a loyalty that forbade thinking, forbade criticism, forbade independence of any sort. Moreover, Colonel House was in contact with a mind much stronger than his, with a personality much more powerful than his. He was caught into the Wilson orbit. He revolved about Mr. Wilson. He got his light from Mr. Wilson, who had that power, which Colonel Roosevelt had, of irradiating minor personalities. Colonel House was nothing until he gravitated to Mr. Wilson. He is going back to be nothing to-day, nothing but a kind, lovable man, a gentle soul rather unfitted for the world, with an extraordinary capacity for friendship and sympathy, and that fine pair of eyes.

I remember at Paris the affecting evidences of the little man's loyalty to his great friend, of whom he could not speak without emotion. He was never tired of dilating upon the wonder of President Wilson's mind.

"I never saw," he would say, "so quick a mind, with such a capacity for instant understanding.

The President can go to the bottom of the most difficult question as no one else in the world can."

House's endless "formulæ" always bore the self-effacing condition, "if Mr. Wilson approves." "If Mr. Wilson approves" was the D. V. of Colonel House's religion. Too much awe of another mind is not good for your own, or carries with it certain implications about your own.

Colonel House's loyalty to Mr. Wilson did not, however, make him hate the men at Paris who stood across the President's path. The personal representative's heart was too catholic for that. He——

> Liked what e're he looked on
> And his looks went everywhere.

He had a kindly feeling for the "old man," Clemenceau. He was a warm friend of Orlando, with whom Mr. Wilson had his quarrel over Fiume. He though well of Lloyd George, whom Mr. Wilson went abroad hating.

The Peace Conference was to him a personal problem. Peace was peace between Wilson and Clemenceau and Lloyd George and Orlando. Compromises were an accommodation among friends.

I never saw a man so utterly distressed as he was when President Wilson threatened to break up the Peace Conference and sent for the George Washington to take him home from Brest. It was as if his own dearest friends had become involved in a violent quarrel. He did not see the incident in terms of the principles involved, but only as the painful interruption of kindly personal relations. Men speak of him sometimes as the one of our commissioners who knew Europe; and Europeans, appreciating his sympathy, have fostered this idea by referring to his understanding of European problems.

But the Europe Colonel House knew was a personal Europe. The countries on his map were Lloyd George, Clemenceau, and Orlando. The problems of his Europe were Lloyd George, Clemenceau, and Orlando. He knew what Lloyd George wanted. He knew what Clemenceau wanted. He knew what Orlando wanted. That was enough.

His kindness of heart, his desire for pleasant personal relations, his incapacity to think in terms of principles, whether of the League of Nations or not, betrayed him in the matter of Shantung. Whether the Peace Conference should return Shantung to China, or leave it to Japan to return to China was to him, he often said, "only a question of method. There is no principle involved." The Japanese were a sensitive people, why should a kind heart question the excellence of their intentions with respect to China? Shantung would of course be returned. It was only a question of how.

The simple heart of Colonel House did not save him, either as a diplomat or as a friend. The failures at Paris plunged Mr. Wilson into depression in which he went as far down into the valley as he had been up on the heights during his vision of a world made better by his hand. In his darker moments he saw nothing but enmity and disloyalty about him—even, a little later, "usurpation" in the case of the timorous and circumspect Mr. Lansing.

Colonel House says that he does not yet know what caused the breach between the President and himself. Relations stopped; that was all.

This is what occurred: Shortly after Colonel House had convinced the President that the disposal of Shantung was only a question of method he disappeared from Paris "to take a rest"; and it became known that after all he was not to sit in the Council of the League of Nations representing America, as Mr. Wilson had originally intended.

At this time, a close friend of President Wilson and one of his most intimate advisers, said to me, "The most insidious influence here is the social influence."

British entertainment of members of the House family had been marked and assiduous, and the flattery had had its effect, though not probably upon the Colonel, who remained unspoiled by social contacts to the last. Nevertheless, a member of Mr. Wilson's family had called the President's attention to the social forces that the British were bringing to bear. The President by this time was in a mood to be made angry and suspicious. Doubt was lodged in his mind. And when he found this country critical of the Shantung settlement, that doubt became a conviction; the British through social attentions, had wheedled House into a position favorable to their allies, the Japanese. The loyal House was convicted of the one unforgivable offense, disloyalty.

When the casting off of House became, later, in this country unmistakable, I inquired regarding it of the friend and adviser of the President whom I have just mentioned, and he repeated to me, forgetting that he used them before, the exact words he had said at Paris, "The most insidious influence at the Peace Conference was the social influence."

The most insidious influence with Colonel House was the kindness of his own heart. He had too many friends. His view of international relations was too personal. Principles will make a man hard, cold, and unyielding, and Colonel House had no principles, or had them only parrot-like from Mr. Wilson. He was the human side of the President, who for those contacts which his office demanded had found a human side necessary and accordingly annexed the amiable Texan.

Wilson's human side had offended him, and he cut it off, accordingly to the scriptural injunction against the offending right hand. The act was cruel, but it was just, as just as the dismissal of Mr. Lansing; for House failed Wilson at Paris, being one of Wilson's greatest sources of weakness there. His excessive optimism, his kindheartedness, his credulity, his lack of independence of mind, his surrender of his imagination to a stronger imagination, his conception of politics not as morals but as the adjustment of personal differences, left Wilson without a capable critical adviser at the Conference.

When House talked to Wilson, it was a weaker

Wilson talking to the real Wilson. Colonel House in retirement and since the breach, is still Colonel House, kindhearted and unobtrusive. He has seen, and he is satisfied. He has a fine and perhaps half-unconscious loyalty to the great man from whose shoulders he surveyed the world. His is an ego that brushes itself off readily after a fall and asks for no alms of sympathy.

He does not, like Mr. Lansing, fill five hundred octavo pages with "I told you so," and you can not conceive of his using that form of self-justification.

I hope to see him some day playing Santa Claus in a children's Christmas celebration at a village church!

© Harris and Ewing

HERBERT CLARK HOOVER

HERBERT HOOVER

ONE reads in the press daily of Hughes and Hoover, or Mellen and Hoover, or Davis and Hoover, or Wallace and Hoover. If it is a question of foreign relations, it is the Secretary of State and Hoover. If it has to do with using our power as a creditor nation to compel the needy foreigners to buy here in spite of the tariff wall we are going to erect against their selling here, it is the Secretary of the Treasury and Hoover. If strikes threaten, it is the Secretary of Labor and Hoover. If the farmers seek more direct access to the markets, it is the Secretary of Agriculture and Hoover.

It is always "and Hoover." What Mr. Hughes does not know about international affairs—and that is considerable—Mr. Hoover does. What Mr. Mellen does not know about foreign finance—and that is less—Mr. Hoover does. What Mr. Davis does not know about labor—and that is everything—Mr. Hoover does. What Mr. Wallace does not know about farm marketing—and that is nothing—Mr. Hoover does.

Herbert Hoover is the most useful supplement of the administration. He possesses a variety of experiences, gained in making money abroad, in administering the Belgian relief, in husbanding the world's food supply after our entrance into the War, in helping write the peace treaty, which no one else equals. He is as handy as a dictionary of dates or a cyclopedia of useful information, invaluable books, which never obtain their just due; for no one ever signs his masterpiece with the name of its coauthor, thus, by "John Smith and the Cyclopedia of Useful Information."

A bad particle to ride into fame behind, that word "and," begetter of much oblivion! Who can say what goes after the "and" which follows the name McKinley, or Hayes, or Cleveland, or even Roosevelt? Who has sufficient "faith in Massachusetts" to remember long the decorous dissyllable connected by "and" with the name Harding? The link, "and," is not strong enough to hold. You recall the "and"; that is all; as in the case of that article of food, origin of many "calories," to use Mr. Hoover's favorite word, in the quick-serve resorts of the humble, where it supplements ably and usefully, but without honorable mention, slender portions of beef, pork, and ham.

To describe briefly, in a phrase, what has happened to Hoover; two years ago, it was "Hoover"; to-day, it is "and Hoover."

Why the connective? Because, to put it bluntly, however great his other gifts are—and they are remarkable—he lacks political intelligence. He reminds one now of a great insect caught in the meshes of a silken web. He struggles this way and that. He flutters his wings, and the web of politics fastens itself to him with a hundred new contacts.

Facing possible elimination from public life, he accepted a dull and unromantic department under Pesident Harding. He was told that he could "make something of it." Modern Greeks bearing gifts always bring you an opportunity which "you, and you alone, can make something of." He is trying to make something of it, something more than Mr. Harding and the party advisers intended when they gave him the Secretaryship of Commerce. He is trying to dramatize some turn of fate and be once more a "big figure." He is tireless. He arrives at his office fabulously early.

Clerks drop in their tracks before he leaves at night. He has time to see everyone who would see him; for he can never tell when "the man with the idea" will knock at his door. Unlike the British naval officer charged with the duty of examining inventions to win the War, who is decribed by Guedalla as sitting like an inverted Micawber "waiting for something to turn down," he is waiting for something to turn up. He does more than wait; he works twenty hours a day trying to turn something up.

And he will turn something up. The chances are that he will do as much for the infant foreign trade of this country as Alexander Hamilton did for the infant finances of this country. He promises to be the most useful cabinet officer in a generation. But this is less than his ambition. If he were an unknown man, it would be enough; but you measure him by the stature of Hoover of the Belgian Relief. Like the issue of great fathers, he is eclipsed by a preceding fame. As well be the son of William Shakespeare as the political progeny of Hoover, The Food Administrator!

The War spoiled life for many men; for Wilson, for Baruch, for Hoover. After its magnificent amplifications of personality, it is hard to descend to every day, and be not a tremendous figure, but a successful secretary of an unromantic department.

He might concentrate with advantage to his future fame. A brief absence from front pages, under the connective "and," would cause the public heart to grow fonder when he did "make something" of his own department.

But two disqualifications stand in his way;—his lack of political intelligence, and his consequent inability to make quick decisions in a political atmosphere. His present diffusion of his energies springs, I think, from indecision; for in politics he can not make up his mind, as he can in business, where the greatest profit lies.

I first heard of this weakness of his when he was Food Administrator in Washington, and when other members of the Wilson War Administration, equal in rank with him and having to coöperate with him, complained frequently of his slowness. He had able subordinates, they said, the leading men in the various food industries, and they had to make up his mind for him. I set this charge down, at the time, to jealousy and prejudice, Mr. Hoover being always an outsider in the Wilson administration; but the long delay and immense difficulty he made over deciding, although all his life a Republican, whether he was or was not a Republican in the campaign of 1920, seemed all the proof of indecision that was needed.

It sounds like heresy about one who has been advertised as he has; but remember that we know little about him except what the best press agents in history have said of him. He achieved his professional success in the Orient, far from observation, and his financial success far from American eyes. His public career in the relief of Belgium and in the administration of food was the object of world-wide good will. And, moreover, indecision in politics is common enough among men who are strong and able in other activities. Mr. Taft was a great judge but wrecked his administration as President by inability to make up his mind. Senator Kellogg was a brilliantly successful lawyer; but in public life he is so hesitant that Minnesota politicians speak of him as "Nervous Nelly," and even Mr. Taft, during the Treaty fight, rebuked him to his face for lack of courage.

Mr. Hoover's face is not that of a decisive character. The brow is ample and dominant; there is vision and keen intelligence; but the rest of the face is not strong, and it wears habitually a wavering self-conscious smile. This smile, as if everybody were looking at him, makes him remind one as he comes out of a Cabinet meeting of a small boy in a classroom carrying a bouquet of flowers up to his teacher. He has, moreover, a strain of pessimism in his nature, which may account for his indecision. You catch him in moods of profound depression. He was in one just before his appointment to the Cabinet, when his European relief work was not going to his liking, and when the politicians, he felt, were forcing him into a position of little scope and opportunity.

In politics, he has enough vanity and self-consciousness to be aware constantly of forces opposed to him, covert, hostile, unscrupulous, personal forces—forces that he does not understand. Give him a mining problem, he can reckon with the forces of nature that have to be overcome. Give him a problem of finance, he knows the enmities of finance. He is in his element. In politics he is not. He is baffled.

An illustrative incident occurred in the spring of 1920, when both parties were talking of him as their candidate for President and he was uncertain whether he was a Republican or not. Mr. Hearst, in his newspapers, published an attack upon him, saying that he was more Briton than American, and to prove it printed a list of British corporations of which he was a director.

All his suspicions were aroused over this everyday occurrence of politics. Where had Mr. Hearst obtained the unfortunate information? He saw plots and treachery. Someone in his confidence must have betrayed him for money. A careful investigation was made, and it was discovered that the editor had drawn upon "Who's Who," to which Mr. Hoover himself had furnished the information before he began thinking of the Presidency.

The politicians tricked him so completely in the preconvention campaign of 1920 that he has the best reasons for distrusting himself. He was always, during that campaign, a candidate for the Republican nomination to the Presidency. At the very time when his spokesman, Julius Barnes, was saying for him that he could not choose between the two parties until he had seen their candidates and read their platforms, and when the Democrats were most seriously impressed with his availability, the manager of his paper in Washington said to me, "This talk of Hoover for the Democratic nomination is moonshine. He won't take it."

"Why not," I asked him.

"Because," he replied, "he does not think it is worth having," a quite practical reason which differed wholly from the official explanation that Mr. Hoover was waiting to see which party was progressive so that he might oppose reaction.

His subsequent support of the more conservative candidate and the more conservative party bore out the truth of what his newspaper manager had said. And in reality, Mr. Hoover is as conservative as Mr. Harding himself, being a large capitalist with all the conservatism of the capitalist class.

A little while ago, Mr. Roosevelt had made it unfashionable to admit that you were conservative. You wished it to be understood that you were open-minded—"forward looking," as Mr. Wilson, who turned reactionary at the test, called it; that you were broad, sympathetic, free from mean prejudices, progressive, in short. Our very best reactionaries of to-day all used to call themselves progressive. Some still do.

The young editor of a metropolitan newspaper, born to great wealth, and imbibing all the narrowness of the second generation, once asked me in those bright days when everybody was thrilling over his "liberality," "Would you call me a radical, or just a progressive?" He was "just a progressive." In a somewhat similar sense, Mr. Hoover was quite unconsciously "just a progressive"—a belated follower of a pleasant fashion, having lived abroad too long when he made his announcement to note the subtle changes that had taken place in our thinking—the rude shock that Russia had given to our "liberality."

But living abroad, it is only fair to add, has created a difference between his conservatism and that, let us say, of Judge Gary. He has grown used to labor unions and even to labor parties, so that they do not frighten him. His is conservatism, none the less, definite conservatism, if more enlightened than the obscurant American variety.

His hesitation and indecision in the spring of 1920 thus did not spring from doubt of the Republican party's progressiveness. He always desired the Republican nomination; but his vanity would suffer by the open seeking of it and the defeat which seemed likely; and his sensitiveness would suffer from the attacks, like that of Mr. Hearst, which an open candidacy would entail; for he is at once vain and thin-skinned.

Springing thus from reluctance to make up his mind, the announcement was received as the evidence of a very large mind. Among the public, Mr. Hoover was taken for a man who cared more for principle than for party or for politics. Among the politicians, he assumed the proportions of a portent, with a genius for politics second only to that of Roosevelt himself, who in a difficult situation could take the one position and say the one thing that might force his nomination.

The Democrats pricked up their ears. Mr. Wilson, sick and discouraged, began to entertain hopes of a candidate who would save the Democracy from ruin. Homer Cummings, National Chairman of Mr. Wilson's party, began to regard Mr. Hoover's possible nomination favorably. The Republican managers became alarmed. They knew from Mr. Hoover's friends that he, as his Washington newspaper manager had said, thought the Democratic nomination not worth having; but they feared lest by the course he was pursuing he might make it worth having, might take it, and might rob them of the election which they felt safely theirs. If they could induce him to declare his Republicanism, the Democrats would drop him, the public would cease to be interested in him as a dramatic personality too big for party trammels, and they themselves could ignore him.

It was decided to have him read out of the Republican party as a warning to him of how he was imperiling his hopes of the only nomination he valued, and at the same time have Republican leaders go to him or his friends and advise him and them that if he would only declare his Republicanism, a popular demand would force his nomination at Chicago.

Senator Penrose was chosen as the Republican whose pontifical damnation would most impress Mr. Hoover. The late W. Murray Crane, whom I have heard described at Mr. Roosevelt's dinner table as "the Uriah Heap of the Republican party," was the emissary who would advise Mr. Hoover to confess the error of his ways and seek the absolution of Penrose. A diary kept at Republican National Headquarters in New York reveals the visits there at the time the plan was made of Mr. Crane and others who took part in the enterprise. Mr. Penrose got up from a sick bed and thundered: under no circumstances would he permit the nomination of Mr. Hoover.

The plot succeeded. In a few days, Mr. Hoover declared that he would not take the Democratic nomination. The Democrats dropped him. The public was bewildered by his finding out that he was a Republican after saying that he could not tell whether he was one or not until he had seen the Republican candidate and the platform.

At the Chicago Convention he received the support of Mr. Crane, Governor Miller, of New York, and, on the last ballot, of William Allen White, who having voted for Harding on the just previous ballot, said he wanted to "leave the bandwagon and ride with the undertaker."

This guilelessness of Mr. Hoover in politics will prevent him from realizing his larger ambitions; but is a source of strength to him in his present position, with American business men who have learned to distrust politicians. At any rate, he is no politician; he thinks as business men think; his interests are their interests; and when he comes to them bearing gifts,—the aid and coöperation of the United States Government in their efforts to win foreign trade,—they do not take him for a Greek.

He possesses great special knowledge which they desire: he knows much about economics and enjoys the advantage of believing that he knows all; he has immense prestige, as a result of all the advertising he received during the War; they come to Washington and sit at his feet like children; he gives them fatherly lectures, even upon the morals of their business, which must be clean, to enter this foreign trade of his, with the Government behind it. They make mental resolutions of reform. To no politician, to no one, even with an instinct for politics, would they listen as they listen to him. He speaks to American business with immense authority. His selection is an example of that unusual instinct for putting the right man in the right place which President Harding has, when he chooses to exercise it.

The post was disappointing to Mr. Hoover; but it was the one in which he will be most useful. Not a lawyer, he would hardly have done for Secretary of State, in spite of his exceptional knowledge of foreign conditions. Not a banker, he lacked the technical equipment for Secretary of the Treasury. Not a politician, he should have, and he has a place in which there are the least possible politics. Mr. Harding denatured him politically by giving him the one business department in the Cabinet. Even Hiram Johnson may come no longer to hate him.

For his present task, besides his special knowledge, his remarkable industry, his tireless application to details, he has one great gift, his extraordinary talent for publicity. There is no one in Washington, not even Mr. Hughes, who knows so well as he does how to advertise what he is doing.

As business recovers and foreign trade develops, the magazine pages will blossom with articles about what American enterprise is achieving in foreign lands, about the coöperation between American business and the American government, and, once more, about Mr. Hoover. Finding markets for American wares all over the earth will be made a romance only second in interest to the feeding of Belgium.

It was not an accident that he was better advertised than any general, admiral, or statesman of the War. It was not all due to the good will of the public, to the work which he did in Belgium and in this country, nor to the extraordinary press agents whose services he was able to command because of that good will. Back of it all was his own instinct for publicity, his sense of what interests the people, his assiduous cultivation of editors and reporters. He has magazine and newspaper contacts only exceeded by those of Roosevelt in his time, and a sense of the power of publicity only exceeded by Roosevelt's.

When he was threatening to win the Democratic nomination for the Presidency in spite of the fact that he was not a Democrat, a supporter of McAdoo complained bitterly to me, "Confound him! He has a genius for self-advertising. He is not half the man McAdoo is. He hasn't McAdoo's courage, optimism, force, or general statesmanship; but he has this infernal talent for getting himself in the papers. There is not much to him but press agenting; but how can you beat that?"

But though his own name has come to count for more than the causes he represents, so that the best way to obtain aid is to ask for it with "Hoover" in big letters and with the suffering children of Central Europe in small letters, still he remains only a name to the American people. They know that he always wears a blue suit of clothes cut on an invariable model, which he adopted years ago. They know that he worked his way through college as a waiter. They know that he grew rich as a mining engineer in the East. That is all. They think of him as a symbol of efficiency, as one who may save their money, as one who may find markets for them and develop their trade, as one who may help the world upon its feet again after the War, as a superman, if you will; but not as a man, not as a human being.

All his advertising has made him appeal to the

American imagination, but not to the American heart. He is a sort of efficiency engineer, installing his charts and his systems into public life,—and who loves an efficiency engineer? There are no stories about him which give him a place in the popular breast. It is impossible to interest yourself in Hoover as Hoover; in Hoover as the man who did this, or the man who did that, or the man who will do this or that, yes,—but not in Hoover, the person.

The reason is that he has little personality. On close contact, he is disappointing, without charm, given to silence, as if he had nothing for ordinary human relations which had no profitable bearing on the task in hand. His conversation is applied efficiency engineering; there is no lost motion, though it is lost motion which is the delight of life. At dinner, he inclines to bury his face in his plate until the talk reaches some subject important to him, when he explodes a few facts, and is once more silent.

Had he a personality with his instinct for publicity, he would be another Roosevelt. But he is a bare expert.

I doubt if he really thinks of human beings as human beings; on the contrary, some engineering graph represents humanity in his mind. It is characteristic of him that he always speaks of the relief of starving populations not in terms of human suffering, but in terms of chemistry. The people, of whatever country he may be feeding, have so many calories now, last month they had so many calories; if they had ten calories more, they could maintain existence. Many times have I heard this formula. It is a weakness in a democracy to think of people in terms of graphs, and their welfare in terms of calories; that is, if you hope to be President of that democracy—not if you are content to be its excellent Secretary of Commerce.

When he came to Washington as a Food Administrator, he brought with him an old associate, a professor from California. A few days later the professor's wife arrived and went to live at the same house where Mr. Hoover and her husband resided. Mr. Hoover knew her well. She and her husband had long been his friends. He met her in the hall, shook hands with her, welcomed her and then lapsed into silence. After some moments, he said, "Well,—" and hesitated.

"Mr. Hoover," she said, "I know you are a busy man. You don't have to stand here trying to think of something to say to me. I know you well enough not to be offended if you don't talk to me at all while I am here."

He laughed and took her at her word. He had the habit of too great relevancy to be human. If he could have said more than "Well" to that woman, he might have been President.

© Harris and Ewing

HENRY CABOT LODGE

HENRY CABOT LODGE

WHEN Henry Cabot Lodge was elected to Congress thirty-four years ago there were no portents in the heavens, but there was rejoicing in his native city of Boston and in many other places. It was hailed as the dawn of a new era. Young, he was only thirty-seven, well educated, a teacher of history, and with six serious books to his credit, he was a new figure in politics; Providence, moving in its mysterious way, had designed him to redeem politics from its baseness and set a shining example.

Everything was in his favor; he was not only learned, so learned, in fact, that he was promptly dubbed the "scholar in politics," but he was rich, and therefore immune from all sordid temptation; he was a gentleman. Mr. Lodge's forbears had been respectable tradesmen who knew how to make money and to keep it—and the latter trait is strongly developed in their senatorial descendant. From them he inherited a fortune; he had been educated in a select private school and then gone through Harvard, whence he emerged with an LL.B. and a Ph.D. attached to his name. By all the established canons he was a "gentleman" as well as a scholar. In the intervals between teaching and writing he had found time to be admitted to the Boston bar.

With that equipment it could be safely predicted Mr. Lodge would go far. He has. To-day he is the leader of the Republican party in the Senate of the United States.

He early justified the promise. While still a Congressional freshman he drafted and introduced into the House the "Force Bill," which came to a violent death in the Senate. That Bill was not only a prophecy but it is a résumé of Mr. Lodge's career. It is partisanship gone mad.

On the pretense that it was intended to secure fair elections in the South, but actually, as described by a member of the House at the time, to prevent elections being held in several districts, it placed the election machinery in the control of the Federal Government, which, through the Chief Supervisor of Elections, to be appointed by the President, and his Prætorian Guard of Deputy Marshals, would have controlled every election and returned an overwhelming Republican majority from the Southern States.

The Bill was typical of Mr. Lodge and the way he plays politics. The Force Bill would probably have ended ingloriously the political career of any other man, but Mr. Lodge had the luck of being a gentleman born in Boston. Boston is slow to forget. A quarter of a century after the Civil War, Boston still remembered that conflict, its heart still bled for the negro deprived of his vote; and a Boston gentleman could do no wrong—to the Democratic Party.

The House amused Mr. Lodge, but it was too promiscuous for a person of his delicate sensibilities who shrank from intimate contact with the uneducated and the socially unwashed. Henry Cabot Lodge always creates the impression that it is a condescension on his part to God to have allowed Him to create a world which is not exclusively possessed by the Cabots and the Lodges and their connections.

All that is only an unfortunate manner. He is really the friend of the people, abominating snobbishness and aristocratic pretensions; in his younger days, when he was campaigning for Congress, he was known to have slapped a constituent

on the back and called him familiarly by his first
name; even now, although he has long ceased to be
a politician and has been canonized as a statesman,
the old impulses are strong in him. When the
time draws near for his reëlection to the Senate,
he goes back to Massachusetts, there to take part
with the common people in their simple pleasures,
and affably to extend a cold and clammy hand to
voters, who still venerate him as a scholar in
politics and a gentleman. So it will be easily
understood why one of Mr. Lodge's temperament
should early have cast his covetous eye on the
Senate, and at the first opportunity moved over to
that more select atmosphere, which he did in 1893.

When Senator Lodge entered public life the
flagrant spoils system was rampant. A little band
of earnest men was fighting to reform the civil
service so as to make it a permanent establishment
with merit and fitness the tests for appointment
instead of political influence. It was a cause naturally to appeal to the "best people" of Boston,
and Mr. Lodge, being one of them, having inflexible principles and a high code of honor, threw
himself eagerly into the reform movement and
became its apostle. His principles were so stern
and unyielding, he demanded such an exalted

standard of private and public morality, that, although he worshipped the Republican Party with a devotion almost as great as the memory of that grandfather who laid the foundation of the family fortunes, with a sorely stricken heart he was compelled to differ with Mr. Blaine and to flirt with those Ruperts of American politics, the Mugwumps.

"The man who sets up as being much better than his age is always to be suspected," says a historian, "and Cato is perhaps the best specimen of the rugged hypocrite that history can produce."

As a summary of the character of Cato, this is admirable, but no one would call Mr. Lodge "rugged."

Mr. Lodge's principles, it has been observed, are inflexible and rest on solid foundation, but like good steel they can bend without breaking. An ardent civil service reformer, a champion of public morality, so long as offices were being awarded to the faithful, he saw no reason why he should be the victim of his own self denying ordinance. Early in his career he became a very successful purveyor of patronage, developing a keen scent for vacant places or a post filled by a Democrat. As a theoretical civil service reformer Mr. Lodge left nothing to be desired; as a practical spoilsman he had few equals. A Senator's usefulness to his friends is much greater than that of a member of the House, and if a Senator works his pull for all that it is worth he can accomplish much. Mr. Lodge was not idle.

With his grandfathers and his fortune Mr. Lodge inherited a violent and bitter dislike of England. Probably no man—not even the most extreme Irish agitator—is more responsible for the feeling existing against England than Mr. Lodge; because the outspoken Irish agitator is known for what he is and treated accordingly; carrying out Mr. Roosevelt's thought, he will be execrated by decent people; but Mr. Lodge, posing as the impartial historian and the patriotic statesman, is applauded.

Just as Mr. Lodge gained a certain fame when he was a member of the House from the Force Bill, which his own party repudiated, so he signalized his admission into the Senate by proposing to force England to adopt free silver. It was an opportunity to strike at England in a vital spot; it was as statesmanlike and patriotic as his attempt to deprive the South of their representatives.

Mr. Cleveland was fighting with splendid courage to save the country from free silver, caring nothing for politics and animated solely by the highest and most disinterested motives, and Mr. Lodge was thinking only of his spite. President Cleveland, said a Boston paper, deserved and had the right to expect Mr. Lodge's support, instead of which "we find our junior Senator introducing a legislative proposition intended to appeal at once to the anti-British prejudices of a good many Americans, and to the desire of the then preponderating sentiment of the country to force a silver currency upon the American people. It was an effort to strike at England."

Mr. Lodge proposed that all imports from Great Britain or her colonies should pay duties double those of the regular rates, and any article on the free list should be made dutiable at thirty-five per cent; these additional and discriminating duties were to remain in force until Great Britain assented to and took part in an international agreement "for the coinage and use of silver."

Mr. Lodge's free silver amendment shared the same tomb with his Force Bill; in the Senate fortunately there were men with broader vision and less passion.

In his biography in the Congressional Directory (written by himself) and in the numerous biographies and sketches which have been published with such frequency (Mr. Lodge has a weakness for seeing himself in print) curiously enough no mention can be found either of the Force Bill or the attempt to coerce England with a silver club. One can only explain this reticence by excessive modesty.

Two years later Mr. Lodge deserted his silver allies and was as enthusiastic in support of the gold standard as he had previously been zealous for the purification of the civil service. A Boston paper said that he "was made to realize, by the influences brought to bear upon him, that he must advocate the gold standard or else provoke the active hostility of the prominent business men of this State." That perhaps is as infamous as anything ever written. That any influences, even those "of the prominent business men of Massachusetts," could cause Mr. Lodge to swerve from his convictions no one will believe. He must have had convictions when he sought to drive England to a silver standard, he must have been convinced that it was for the good of the United States as well as the whole world, he must have satisfied himself, for Mr. Lodge never permits his emotions to control his intelligence, that his action was wise and patriotic. But although Mr. Lodge will not surrender his convictions he has no scruples about consistency.

Mr. Lodge's principles are so stern that he refused to consent to Colombia being paid for the territory seized by President Roosevelt. Mr. Lodge made a report (this was when Mr. Wilson was President, and I mention it merely as an historical fact) in which he denounced Colombia's claim as blackmail, resented it as an insult to the memory of Mr. Roosevelt, and delared in approved copybook fashion (being fond of platitudes), that friendship between nations cannot be bought. Later (this was when Mr. Harding was President, and I mention it merely as an historical fact) as Chairman of the Committee on Foreign Relations, he brought in a report urging the ratification of the treaty, and discovered that Mr. Roosevelt had really been in favor of the treaty, expunged the unpleasant word blackmail from his lexicon, and sapiently observed, so impossible is it for him not to indulge in platitudes, that sometimes a nation has to pay more for a thing than it is really worth; a reflection that would have done credit to the oracular wisdom of Captain Jack Bunsby.

Mr. Lodge attacked the treaty of peace with

137

Germany while it was still in process of negotiation and severely criticized Mr. Wilson for not having consulted the Senate. That the Senate has
no right to ask about the details of a treaty before
the President sends it in for ratification is a con-
stitutional axiom which Mr. Lodge, with his customary mental infidelity, caressed at one time and
spurned at another.

When the treaty with Spain was before the
Senate (that was when Mr. McKinley was President, and I mention it merely as an historical fact)
it was attacked by some of the Democrats. To
silence these criticisms Mr. Lodge said, "We have
no possible right to break suddenly into the middle
of a negotiation and demand from the President
what instructions he has given to his representatives. That part of treaty making is no concern
of ours."

The Democrats attempted to defeat the ratification of the treaty, and if that was done, said Mr.
Lodge, "we repudiate the President and his action
before the whole world, and the repudiation of the
President in such a matter as this is, to my mind,
the humiliation of the United States in the eyes of
the civilized world." The President could not be sent
back to say to Spain "with bated breath" (even in

his most solemn moments Mr. Lodge cannot resist the commonplace) "we believe we have been too victorious and that you have yielded us too much and that I am very sorry that I took the Philippines from you."

But that was precisely what Mr. Lodge demanded should and must be done when Mr. Wilson brought back the peace treaty. Inconsistency, as I have before remarked, Mr. Lodge cares nothing about, but his patriotism and partisanship are so inextricably intertwined that it is always difficult to discover whether in his loftiest flights it is the patriot who pleads or the partisan who intrigues.

Thus, in the debate on the Spanish treaty, Mr. Lodge delivered himself of these noble sentiments: "I have ideals and beliefs which pertain to the living present, and a faith in the future of my country. I believe in the American people as they are to-day and in the civilization they have created," and many more beautiful words to the same effect. It was the language of a statesman with aspirations and convictions. It sounded splendidly. Mr. Lodge is a classical scholar, and one wonders whether he remembers his Epictetus: "But you utter your elegant words only from your lips; for this reason they are without strength and dead, and it is nauseous to listen to your exhortations and your miserable virtue; which is talked of everywhere."

It was the late Senator Wolcott, one of the most brilliant orators of his day, who explained why Mr. Lodge's oratory left men cold. Wolcott was commenting on a speech delivered by Lodge a few days earlier and someone said to him that men listened to Lodge with eyes undimmed.

"To bring tears from an audience," said Wolcott, "the speaker must feel tears here (and he pointed to his throat), but Lodge can speak for an hour with nothing but saliva in his throat."

Mr. Lodge's dislike of Mr. Wilson was almost malignant. Rumor ascribes it to professional jealousy. Before Mr. Wilson came into prominence Mr. Lodge was the only scholar in politics, but Mr. Wilson was so far his superior in erudition, especially in Mr. Lodge's chosen profession of history, that he resented being deprived of his monopoly. Perhaps there is another reason. Mr. Lodge has cherished two ambitions, neither of which has been gratified. The Presidency has been the *ignis fatuus* he has pursued; he was the residuary legatee of Mr. Roosevelt's bankrupt political estate in 1916, it will be recalled; last year, after his fight on the treaty, he considered himself the logical candidate and believed he had the nomination in his grasp. He has longed to be Secretary of State, and it was a bitter disappointment when Mr. Harding did not invite him to enter the Cabinet.

Mr. Lodge is a curious and not uninteresting study in psychology. He has no great talent, but he is not without some ability; in his youth he was an industrious plodder and fond of study. He has read much but absorbed little; he is well educated in the narrow sense of the schoolmaster, but he has no philosophic background; his is the parasitic mind that sucks sustenance from the brains of others and gives nothing in return. He is without the slightest imagination and is devoid of all sense of humor; and without these two, imagination, which is the gift of the poet, and humor, which is the dower of the philosopher, no man can see life whole.

He has genius almost for misunderstanding public sentiment. To him may be applied Junius' characterization of the Duke of Grafton: "It is not that you do wrong by design, but that you should never do right by mistake."

With all these defects, the defects of heritage

141

and environment and temperament, so much was expected from Mr. Lodge, and so much he might have done, that it is a disappointment he has accomplished so little. He has been thirty-four years in Congress, and his career can be summed up in three achievements—the Force Bill, the attempt to wreck England by driving her to silver coinage, and the part he took in defeating the treaty of peace with Germany. The Force Bill and the silver amendment his biographers have charitably forgotten; will the future biographer deal as gently with the closing years of his life? And if so, what material will the biographer have?

Macaulay, reviewing Barère's Memoirs—and allowing for the difference in time and manners and morals there is a strange similarity between the leader of the French Revolution and the leader of the Senate—said, "We now propose to do him, by the blessing of God, full and signal justice."

We think we may say, with proper humility, that, by the blessing of God, we have done Senator Henry Cabot Lodge full and signal justice.

BERNARD MANNES BARUCH

BERNARD M. BARUCH

A CLEVER woman magazine writer once asked Bernard M. Baruch for some information about the peace treaty. The question was not in his special field, the economic sections of the treaty, and he told her so.

"It took him one sentence to say that he could not tell me what I wanted to know," she described the interview afterward. "And then he talked to me for two hours about himself. He told me of his start in life as a three-dollar-a-week clerk, how rich he was, his philosophy of life; how you should recognize defeat when it was coming, accept it before it was complete and overwhelming and start out afresh, how liberal and advanced were his social views, how with all his wealth he was ready to accept a capital tax as perhaps the best way out of the bog in which the war had left the world, how democratic he was in his relations with his employees and his servants. It all seemed as amazing to him as if he were describing someone else, or as if it had just happened the day before."

Perhaps it is only to women and to journalists that men talk so frankly about themselves, to the most romantic and best trained listening sex and profession, who perforce survey the heights from below. But this young woman's experience was, I have reason to believe, a common one.

Is it vanity? You say that a man who talks so much about himself must be vain. To conclude that he is vain is not to understand Mr. Baruch. Is a child vain when it brings some little childish accomplishment, some infantile drawing on paper, and delightedly and frankly marvels at what he has done? It is given to children and to the naïve openly to wonder at themselves without vanity, with a deep underlying sense of humility, and in Mr. Baruch's case the unaffected delight in himself proceeds from real humility.

After twenty-five years in the jungle of Wall Street, there is—contradictions multiply in his case—much of the child about Mr. Baruch, simple, trustful—outside of Wall Street,—incapable of concealment,—outside of Wall Street—of that which art has taught the rest of us to conceal. His humility makes him wonder; his naïveté makes him talk quite frankly, unrestrained by the conventions that balk others. After all, is not wondering at yourself a sign of humility? A vain man, become great by luck, by force of circumstances, by the possession of gifts which he does not himself fully understand, would still take himself for granted. He would not be a romance to himself, but a solid, unassailable fact.

For Baruch the great romance is Baruch, the astonishing plaything of fate, who started life as a three-dollar-a-week broker's clerk; made millions, lost millions, made millions again, lost millions again; finally, still young, quit Wall Street with a fortune that left the game of the market dull and commonplace, seeking a new occupation for his energies; became during the war next to the President, the most powerful man in Washington; emerged from the war, which wrecked most reputations, with a large measure of credit, prepared by the amazing past for an equally amazing future. A career like that makes it impossible for the man who knows it best not to expect anything. Why not the "Disraeli of America?"—a phrase he once, rather confidentially, employed concerning his anticipated future.

Did you ever see a portrait bust smiling, not

softly with the eyes or with a slight relaxation of the mouth, but firmly, definitely, lastingly smiling, with some inward source of satisfaction? Look at Jo Davidson's bust of Baruch, among the famous men at the Peace Conference.

I once saw the various sketches in clay that went to the making of that portrait—the subject was proving elusive to the sculptor. There were two obvious traits to be represented; the unusual knot in the brow between the eyes and the smile, without which it was evident that you had not Baruch. The extraordinary concentration in the forehead was easy enough to transfer to clay; but the smile kept defying the artist. When a smile was traced in the clay it softened the face out of character, destroyed that intensity which the central massing of the brow denoted; and when the smile was deleted the face lost all its brilliance, became merely intense, concentrated, racial, acquisitive perhaps, clearly not Mr. Baruch's face. Ultimately the sculptor succeeded in wedding a smile to that brow, and the bust went on exhibition with those of Wilson, Foch, House, Clemenceau, and the others; but the union was never more than a compromise, a marriage of convenience for the artist.

That smile is as inevitable a part of Baruch as his

engaging naïveté in talking about himself. It is
always there, brilliant, unrelated to circumstances.
It does not spring from a sense of humor,—Mr.
Baruch, like the rest of the successful, has not a
marked sense of humor; a sense of the irony of fate
he has, perhaps, but not more. It does not denote
gaiety, nor sympathy, nor satire; it is not kind nor
yet unkind; it does not relax the features, which
remain tense as ever even when smiling; it suggests
satisfaction, self-confidence, and a secret inner
source of contentment. It is with Mr. Baruch when
he is tired, or ought to be tired; the romance of
Baruch is an internal spring of refreshment. It
does not leave him when he is angry, if he is ever
angry; the romance of Baruch diverts him. Though
always there, it is not a fixed smile, a mask, something worn for the undoing of Wall Street; it is a
real smile. Somewhere subconsciously there abides
the picture of the poor clerk become amazingly
rich, of power in Washington, of a beckoning future
with possibilities as extraordinary as the wonders of
the past. Life is not logical, dull, commonplace, a
tissue of cause and effect; it proceeds delightfully
by daily miracles. The American Disraeli is no
further away to-day than was the Baruch of to-day
from the Baruch of yesterday. Enough to account

for a smile in marble, bronze, or in whatever metal the human face is made of.

Take the miracle of the War Administration. It was not vanity but humility, the kind of humility that would have saved Wilson, that served Mr. Baruch there. He came to Washington out of Wall Street and Wall Street is always anathema. More than that he came out of that part of Wall Street which is beyond the pale; he did not belong to the right monied set there; which is to be anathema with that part of the community to which Wall Street itself is not anathema; moreover he had been unjustly accused in connection with the famous Wall Street "leak." And he entered an administration which was the center of much prejudice and hatred. Yet he was modest enough, however, to assume that his personality did not count, that it was the work to be done which mattered, and that he could depend upon the friendliness both of the Republicans and of the great industrial interests of the country to that work if it should be properly done.

The belief Mr. Wilson has and a much lesser man, Hiram Johnson, has, that men are thinking exclusively about them personally and not about the causes they advocate or the measures they propose is a more dangerous form of vanity than the habit of admiring oneself audibly. It requires collossal egotism to imagine the existence of many enemies and Mr. Baruch is genuinely humble in the matter of enmity. After watching him during the war, in an administration which was enemy mad, I fancy he counts his genuine foes on the fingers of one hand. Moreover he was quite impersonal about his task. He did not do everything himself on the theory that no one else was quite big enough to do it. There is no practical snobbism about him. His knowledge of the industries of the country was that of the speculator; it was not that of the practical industrialist, and he knew it.

He surrounded himself with the best men he could find. He trusted them implicitly, his habit being not to distrust men until he finds that they can be trusted but to trust them unless he finds that they cannot be trusted—also a modest and naïve trait. He was never tired of praising Legg, Replogle, Somers, and the other business men whom he brought to Washington, praising himself, of course, for his skill in choosing them—he never achieves self-forgetfulness—but giving them full credit for the work of the War Industries Board. And he inspired an extraordinary loyalty among his associates, big and little. He treated the Republicans as he treated big business as if all had only one interest, above politics and personalities, and that was to win the war. And when President Wilson, in response to Republican criticism of the war organization, gave him real power to mobilize American industry, the Republicans applauded the bestowal of authority as constructive and took credit to themselves for accomplishing it.

Baruch and Hoover, alone of the business men who came to Washington during the war achieved real successes in the higher positions, and he showed vastly the greater capacity of the two to operate in a political atmosphere. A man who was nothing but a Wall Street speculator, not an industrial organizer, organized successfully the biggest industrial combination the world has ever seen; a man who was suspect of American business got on admirably with American business, and a man who had not been in politics accomplished the impossible task of adjusting himself to work under political conditions. It is another chapter in the romance of Baruch.

He cannot explain it, so why should not he wonder about it quite openly and quite delightedly, with all his engaging naïveté? That inability to explain anything is one of the characteristics of Mr. Baruch. When you begin to apprehend it you begin to see why he is a romance to himself. He cannot explain himself to himself, nor to anyone else, no matter how much he tries. And even more, he cannot explain his opinions, his conclusions, his decisions to anyone in the world with all the words at his command. He can never give reasons. Mentally nature has left him, after a manner, *incommunicado*. His mind does not proceed as other men's minds do.

The author of the *Mirrors of Downing Street* describes Lord Northcliffe's mind as "discontinuous." If I had never talked to Lord Northcliffe I should be led to suppose that his mind resembled Mr. Baruch's. But the British journalist's mental operations are a model of order and continuity compared to those of the former American War Industries Chairman. Like the heroes of the ancient poems Mr. Baruch's mind has the faculty of invisibility. You see it here; a moment later you see it there, and for the life of you cannot tell how it got from here to there, a gift of incalculability which must have been of great service in Wall Street, but which does not promote understanding nor communication. And the more Mr. Baruch tries to give you the connecting links between here and there the worse off you are, both of you.

The ordinary mind is logical and is confined within the three dimensions of the syllogism. You watch it readily enough shut in its little cage whose walls are the major premise, the minor premise, and the conclusion. There is no escape as we say, from the conclusion. There is no escape anywhere.

But Mr. Baruch's mind escapes easily. It possesses the secret of some fourth mental dimension, known only to the naïve and the illogical, or perhaps supralogical. He has brilliant intuitions, hunches, premonitions, the acute perceptions of some two or three extra senses that have been bred or schooled out of other men.

Perhaps he is like Lloyd George, who is not logical but achieves his successes through two or three senses which ordinary men have not; however, unlike Lloyd George, he cannot simulate logic and, after jumping to his conclusions, reduce them to the understanding of the three-dimensional mind. It is a grief to him that he cannot; for if he could make a speech, that is to say, translate himself, that figure of Disraeli would, he thinks, be less remote. But when your mental operations are a succession of miracles, you may have brilliant intuitions and extraordinary prevision about the mineral supplies necessary to win the war,—which he had—you may have wonder, like the naïve and the poets, about that extraordinary thing yourself, or about that still more extraordinary thing which is life or destiny, but you cannot move the masses.

Still there are compensations. A perfectly logical mind would have explained all the wonder away, reduced the miracle of personality to a stolid operation of cause and effect, quite self-approbatively no doubt, and made Mr. Baruch talk of himself as the rest of the great do, modestly, after this fashion: "Behold me! I am what I am because when I was nine years old I saved nine cents and resolved then and there always to save as many cents each year as I was years old. Young man, *save !*"

There is no fun in being not a wonder but a copy book. And a perfectly logical mind would flirt with Disraeli warily. It would say, "One does not at fifty change from business to politics with success. Disraeli didn't start out in Wall Street. As the Germans say, 'what will become vinegar sours early.'"

Mr. Baruch slips easily through the three sides

of this reasoning. Life is not logical. Fate is not logical. He is not logical.

He has had his taste of public life under Wilson and he wants more. I venture to say that he would give every one of his many millions and be as poor, well, poorer than any member of the present cabinet, to be in the place Mr. Hughes occupies to-day.

Everyone who knows him has heard him say that when he entered office he resolved to quit business because he learned so much as head of the War Industries Board that it would be improper for him ever to go into the market again. There is more to it than that; public life has given him a profound distaste for mere money-making. He wrote to Senator Kenyon the other day that he had not made a dollar since he went to work for the government. I believe that to be true for I have found him an extraordinarily truthful and honest man. He has that desire for public distinction which is so often characteristic of his race. He has the idealism, a characteristic also of the race which gave to the world two great religions. He has the same passion for public service now that he once had for the market. And he belongs to a race, which, in spite of all our national catholicity on the subject of races, has never yet produced its Disraeli in America, and to a party out of power, perhaps for a long time, and he spent his youth learning a trade which is not the trade he would follow now.

All of this accounts for his restlessness. He is still youthful and has enormous energies and no occupation for them. He loves personal publicity and has an instinct for it, not so keen as Hoover's or Will H. Hays', but still keen.

Whither shall he turn? To the organization of his party? There he may buy the right to be lampooned and in the end, if his party succeeds, to be introduced into the Cabinet apologetically, as Hays and Daugherty were, on the plea that the President must appoint a number of party workers. To the Senate? It is a body which affords escape from the boredom of small town life for men who have grown rich on the frontier or in the dull Middle West. It carries with it an excuse to live in Washington, some social position there, and a title envied in Marion, Reno, Butte, or Salt Lake City. Senators who start young serve long and obediently, suppressing all their natural instincts for self-expression, and attain if they are lucky the scant distinction of a committee chairmanship in a legislature that has steadily tended toward submergence. To the House? Individuals are lost in the House. And the Presidency comes to few, and by chance.

Knowing his ambition for public distinction and his wealth, men go to him every day to sell him the road to power and influence, and, if you will, public service. Let him have the Democratic organization on condition of paying its debts and financing its activities. One faction of the Democratic party recently sought control, spreading the understanding that Mr. Baruch would, in the event of its success, open wide his pocket book. After the meeting of the National Committee at which this faction met its defeat I said to a prominent member of the victorious group: "Now that you have won you will probably get Baruch's money. He is restless, eager to find an outlet for his energies, less interested in any personality than in his party. Hang on and wait and he must come to you."

"Do you know," he replied, lowering his voice confidentially, "That is just the way I diagnose it."

And at this very time the Republicans, hearing much of Mr. Baruch's money and its use to build up such an intensive organization for the Democrats, as Chairman Hays with a million or two at his disposal had erected for them, considered

seriously whether or not it would not be wise themselves to occupy Mr. Baruch's energies and divert
his ambitions away from party organization. They
debated putting Mr. Baruch on the commission to
reorganize the executive departments of the government. All had their eyes on the same ambition
and the same wealth!

Several daily newspapers in New York, and I
know not how many magazines and weeklies, have
been offered at one time or another to Mr. Baruch,
for it is known that one of his ideas of public service
is to own and edit a great liberal journal, a "Manchester Guardian" of America. But an opportunity to buy a newspaper in New York is an opportunity to invest $3,000,000 or $4,000,000, to lose
$500,000 or more for several years thereafter and
to become the national figure that Mr. Ochs is, or
Mr. Reid is, or Mr. Munsey is, certainly something
far short of the American Disraeli or even the
Baruch of the War Industries Board.

Mr. Baruch, you will observe, has no vulgar
illusions about what money will buy. He likes
money. It brings with it a certain personal enlargement. It adds to the romance of himself in
his own eyes, as well as in the eyes of others. It
procures the flattering ears of journalists, and a

place on front pages, and, if one inclines toward ostentation, even the ownership of a newspaper itself.

But money will not buy a commanding place in public life. And even if it would buy such a place he would not be content to do other than earn one. He wants to repeat the thrills of his youth in the market, in the thrills of a second youth in Washington. He is incurably romantic.

To sum him all up in a sentence—he has an extraordinary sense of wonder and an unequalled sense of reality, the sense of wonder directed toward himself, the sense of reality directed largely but not exclusively elsewhere.

ELIHU ROOT

ELIHU ROOT

ELIHU ROOT might have been so much publicly and has been so little that a moral must hang somewhere upon his public career.

He might have been many things. He might have been President of the United States if his party ever could have been persuaded to nominate him. He might have been one of the great Chief Justices of the Supreme Court if a President could have been persuaded to appoint him. He might have given to the United States Senate that weight and influence which have disappeared from it, if he had had a passion for public service. He might have been Secretary of State in the most momentous period of American foreign relations if a certain homely instinct in Mr. Harding had not led him to prefer the less brilliant Mr. Hughes. He might have made history. But he has not. Out of his eight years in the Cabinet and six years in the Senate nothing constructive came that will give his

Senators did oppose Mr. Root, but their lack of influence with the President has been sufficiently exposed by events.

The real obstacle to Mr. Root's appointment was Mr. Harding's distrust of him, the instinctive feeling of a simple direct nature against a mind too quick, too clever, too adroit, too invisible in many of its operations. Mr. Harding, being commonplace himself, likes a more commonplace kind of greatness than Mr. Root's. Those who were close to him said the President feared that Mr. Root would "put something over on him." A certain moral quality in Mr. Hughes outweighed Mr. Root's special experience and wider reputation.

Mr. Roosevelt used to tell a story boastfully of his own practicality which throws much light on Mr. Root and upon the reason for Mr. Root's comparative failure as a public man.

"When I took Panama," he would say, "I found all the members of my Cabinet helpful except one. Mr. Root readily found numerous precedents. Mr. Taft was sympathetic and gave every assistance possible. Mr. Knox alone was silent. At last I turned to him in the Cabinet meeting and I said, 'I should like to hear from the Attorney General on the legality of what we are doing.' Mr.

Knox looked up and said, 'Mr. President, if I were you I should not have the slightest taint of legality about the whole affair.'"

Such was Mr. Root. Public questions always were likely to occur to him first as exercises in mental adroitness rather than as moral problems. His extremely agile mind finds its chief pleasure in its own agility. Then he was always the advocate, always instinctively devoting himself to bolstering up another man's cause for him.

"He is a first class second," said Senator Penrose, objecting to him as a candidate for President at the Republican Convention of 1916, "but he is not his own man."

He is always someone else's mouthpiece and publicly he is chiefly remembered as Mr. Roosevelt's mouthpiece. When he came to New York and made the speech that elected Hughes Governor and made possible Hughes as Secretary of State he said, "I speak for the President." He equally spoke for the President when he delivered that other remembered address, warning the States that unless they mended their ways the Federal Government would absorb their vitality.

The law is a parasitic profession and Mr. Root's public career is parasitic. He lacks originality, he lacks passion—there is no p.ace for passion in that clear mind—he lacks force. He elucidates other men's ideas, works out or puts into effect their policies, presents their case, is, by temperament, by reason of gifts amounting almost to genius, of defects that go with those gifts always and everywhere, the lawyer. His public career has been controlled by this circumstance.

I doubt if he ever had a real love of public life. He turned to it late, after he had made his success in the profession of his choice, and he carried over into it the habits of the law. He always seemed to be taking cases for the public. He took a case for Mr. McKinley as Secretary of War because the War Department needed reorganization and the case promised to be interesting. He took a case for Mr. Roosevelt as Secretary of State because Mr. Roosevelt was the most interesting client in the world. He took a case for New York State, to remodel its constitution, a case that ended disastrously. He took a case for Mr. Wilson in Russia and another, the League of Nations, to form its international court for it. He was willing to take a case for Mr. Harding to make a going concern of the world for him following the smash-up of the war, something like the task of counsel of a receivership, the most interesting receivership of all time.

For a few years Mr. Roosevelt made public life interesting to Mr. Root who, it looked then, might devote the rest of his career to national affairs.

It was a sparkling period for America. We have never had an "age" in the history of this country like the age of Elizabeth or the age of Louis XIV, or the age of Lorenzo, the Magnificent; time is too short and democracy too rigid for such splendors; but the nearest equivalent to one was the "age," let us call it that, of Theodore Roosevelt. There was the central figure—an age must have a central figure—a buoyant personality with a Renaissance zest for life, and a Renaissance curiosity about all things known, and unknown, and a boundless capacity for vitalizing everyone and everything with which he came in contact.

Dull moments were unknown. Knighthood was once more in flower, wearing frock coats and high hats and reading all about itself in the daily press. Lances were tilted at malefactors of great wealth, in jousts where few were unhorsed and no blood spilled. Fair maidens of popular rights were rescued; great deeds of valor done. Legends were created, the legend of Leonard Wood, somewhat damaged in the last campaign, the legend of the Term's Cabinet, with its Garfields and its Pinchots, now to be read about only in the black letter books of the early twentieth century, and the legend of Elihu Root, still supported in a measure by the evidences of his highly acute intelligence, but still like everything else of those bright days, largely a legend.

Roosevelt, the Magnificent, made men great with a word, and his words were many. His great were many likewise, great statesmen, great public servants, great writers, great magazine editors, great cowboys from the West, great saints and great sinners, great combinations of wealth and great laws to curb them; everything in scale and that a great scale. Mr. Root acquired his taste for public life in that "age" just as Mr. Hoover, Mr. Baruch and a dozen others did theirs in the moving period of the Great War. It is easy to understand how.

Like all remarkable ages this age was preceded by discoveries. The United States had just fought a war which had ended in a great victory, over Spain. The American people were elated by their achievement, aware of their greatness, talked much and surely of "destiny," the period in Washington being but a reflection of their own mood. Their mental horizon had been immensely widened by the possession, gained in the war, of some islands in the Pacific whose existence we had never heard of before.

Until that time there had been for us only two nations in the world, the United States and England, the country with which we had fought two wars, and innumerable national campaigns. Historically there had of course been another country as friendly as England had sometimes been inimical, France, but France had ceased to be a nation and became a succession of revolutions.

Manila Bay had been a series of revelations, besides teaching us that Philippines is spelled with two "ps" and only one "l." We had there discovered Germany, a country whose admirals had bad sea manners. We knew at once that our next war would be with Germany, although the day before Dewey said, "You may fire when you are ready, Gridley," we would as soon have thought that our next war would be with Patagonia.

There too we had an interesting and surprising experience with England, hitherto known chiefly for her constant designs on the national dinner pail. She behaved in striking and pleasing contrast with

Germany. Blood, on that bright day, May 1, 1898, began to be thicker than water. Learning once more had come out of the East. From Manila Bay flowed such a tide of new ideas, such a reassessment of old conceptions as had not visited the world since the discovery of Greek and Latin letters put an end to the Middle Ages.

Perceiving our widened interest, John Hay, as Secretary of State, took our foreign relations on a grand Cook's tour of the world. He showed us Europe and the Orient. In honor of Manila Bay he invented that brilliant fiction, the "open door" in the East. Turning our attention to the world we discovered the General Staff. Hitherto our army had fought mostly with the scattered Indian tribes of the West and you cannot use a General Staff in conducting six separate wars at once, each no bigger than a good-sized riot. But as Admiral Perry had opened the eyes of the Hermit Kingdom of Japan, so Admiral whatever-his-name-was who consented to be sunk by Dewey, the unremembered hero of this great enlightenment, had opened the eyes of this Hermit Republic of the West to the world across the seas.

We had to have a General Staff. Mr. Root, as Secretary of War, gave us one, faithfully copied from the best European models. Roosevelt, the Magnificent, stood by and said "Bully." Everything was of this order; so it was to a tremendously interesting job that Mr. Root succeeded when he took the place of John Hay as Secretary of State. The mood of the hour was expansive and a luminous personality pervaded the national life.

But public service cannot always be so interesting as it is at its fullest moments. The luminous personality went out. And Mr. Root's next experience, in the United States Senate, was disillusioning.

The Senate is a body in which you grow old, ungracefully waiting for dead men's shoes. The infinite capacity for taking pains which Senators have is not genius. If the gods have been good to you, as they were to Henry Cabot Lodge, you enter the upper house young, a scholar and idealist, with the hope of the Presidency as the reward of generous service. Where the race is to the slow you lay aside your winged gifts one by one and your ambition centers finally not on the Presidency but on some committee chairmanship clung to by a pertinacious octogenarian.

Hope deferred makes you avaricious of little favors, until when a British journalist writes of you as one did of Henry Cabot Lodge, making his speech before the last Republican national convention at Chicago, that you "looked like an elderly peer addressing a labor gathering," your cup of happiness, is full to the brim, as Henry Cabot Lodge's was,—whether because you are compared to a lord or because other people, lesser than Senators, are put into their proper inferior place. Mr. Lodge is the perfect flower of the Senate. It is a flower that does not bloom in a night. It is almost a century plant.

Into this Senate came Mr. Root, full stature, as he might walk into the Supreme Court of the United States, preceded by his reputation. On Olympus one may spring full grown like Minerva from the head of Jove. But not in the Senate, where strong prejudice exists against any kind of cerebral generation. A young Senator from Ohio, Mr. Harding, arrived in the upper House early enough to see the portent of Mr. Root there. He keeps to this day a sense of its unbecomingness.

From his desk on the floor Mr. Root talked to the country, but the Senate did not listen. One does not speak in the Senate by the authority of intellect or of personality. One speaks by the authority of dead men's shoes.

Not being a big committee chairman, Mr. Root was not of counsel in the big cases. He tried to associate himself with counsel but the traditions of the Senate and the jealousy of Senators were against him. He had not the passion for public service that makes Reed Smoot and Wesley Jones miraculously patient with the endless details of legislation. After six years he quit.

"I am tired of it," he said to Senator Fall, "the Senate is doing such little things in such a little way." It was different from public life under Roosevelt where one did not notice size of what they did—one has not yet noticed the size of what they did—for the grandeur of the way they did it.

I have said that Mr. Root's mind with its advocate's bent always occupied itself with the justification of other men's views, his chief's or his party's. There was one notable exception, his break with the Republicans while he was in the Senate on the question of discriminating in favor of American shipping through the Panama Canal. A clever lawyer's argument can be made that when the United States said "all nations" in its treaty with Great Britain regarding the Canal it meant all nations except itself. But Mr. Root declined to make it, holding that plain morality and a greater respect for the obligations of a treaty than Bethman Hollweg expressed when he called them scraps of paper required this country to charge just the same tolls for American ships using the canal as for British ships or any other ships using it.

The general Republican argument is that thus interpreted, the Hay-Pauncefote treaty is so foolish and so inconvenient a treaty that Mr. Hay must not have meant what he said when he wrote it, and really did mean something that he wholly failed to say. The reasons for contending that Mr. Hay meant no tolls for the United States and tolls for England, when he wrote the same tolls for everybody are highly ingenious and as it was a Democratic President who was asserting that Mr. Hay used language in its ordinary sense, Mr. Root as a Republican might have been expected to declare that Mr. Hay used it in quite the reverse of its ordinary sense. But he did not. He supported the Democratic President and treated the Republican position as if it had not the slightest taint of legality in it, to the lasting shock of Mr. Harding, on whose side the precedents are, for nations do say "all nations," and are later found to mean all nations but themselves when their virtuous promises to make no exceptions in their own favor turn out to be inconvenient.

When Mr. Root took a high moral stand on the treaty it was said among Republican Senators that he was thinking more of the transcontinental railroads which were fighting competition by water than he was of the sanctity of international engagements. The probability is that he was probably thinking more of John Hay and Elihu Root than he was of either. He was in the Cabinet when John Hay as Secretary of State made the treaty. Senator Lodge, the only other Senator to agree with Mr. Root and disagree with his party about the meaning of all nations, was John Hay's closest friend. Probably both of them, intimately associated with Mr. Hay, had their part in the making of the treaty. They had perhaps the sensitiveness of authors about their capacity to say exactly what they meant. They wanted to recognize their own international piece when it was put on the stage by the commercially minded producers of the Senate.

The history of the Hay-Pauncefote treaty is interesting and unfamiliar. Attaching Pauncefote's name to the treaty was a delicate act of international courtesy since there is Pauncefote's

word for it, privately spoken, that he had nothing
to do with the writing of it.

Hay draughted the treaty by himself probably
with the cognizance of Root and Lodge, the great
lawyer who was his associate in the Cabinet and his
closest personal friend in the Capitol. Hay then
handed it to Pauncefote, the British minister here.
Pauncefote transmitted it to the foreign office in
London which received it with surprise and probably with satisfaction, for the Clayton-Bulwer
treaty which it in a sense revived, had been forgotten for nearly half a century. Delay is the rule
of foreign offices.

Perhaps Mr. Hay's treaty was not so generous
as it seemed on first reading, a suspicion which
seems to have been justified by the interpretation
put upon it by the final authority upon international engagements, the Republican National
Convention at Chicago. And if it was as generous
as it seemed let not America think Great Britain
too eager in accepting it, let America pay a little to
overcome the reluctance of Great Britain in setting
her approval upon the new contract.

At last, after much apparent hesitation, the
foreign office agreed to the new treaty in consideration of America's throwing in with it an arbitra-

tion of the Bering Sea dispute. President Roosevelt interpreted Mr. Hay's arbitration contract
much as the Republican National Convention
interpreted Mr. Hay's treaty, by appointing American arbitrators who promised beforehand, in giving
a fair and impartial hearing to the Canadian claims,
always to vote for the American position and to
resign and be succeeded by others if they found
that they could not do so.

Why, then, the prevailing distrust of Mr. Root?

His public morals regarding the Hay-Pauncefote
treaty were better than those of his party, even if
we accept the view that they were dictated by
nothing more than a certain mental integrity, a
certain consistency with himself. He was as virtuous in the taking of the Panama Canal as the
virtuous Mr. Roosevelt. He had the advocate's
honesty of being true to his client, whether his
client was the public or the great corporations.
Mentality was uppermost in him, so that he took
primarily a logical rather than a moral view of all
questions; but also so much that he could not pre-
tend, could not act, and thus he was more honest
than the politicians.

His statesmanship was discontinuous, being an
interesting avocation rather than a career. Of it

little has been permanent. His General Staff soon lapsed into incompetence; if it had not, it might have been the danger to American national life that the German General Staff was to German national life. Recently it was merged with the high command. As Secretary of State he was not creative, Mr. Harding turning back to the solid ground of American international policy, rested upon John Hay's open door and Knox's dollar diplomacy. Root in foreign relations merely succeeded with the Senate where Hay had failed. Always the advocate, he takes other men's ideas, Hay's or Wilson's and justifies them or makes them practical. His New York constitution failed, being unjustly suspected. His world court has little better hope of acceptance, for Mr. Hughes is not a voluntary sharer of glory.

In spite of it all, some greatness remains, the impression of a powerful though limited intelligence. His career was to give us a moral. It is: if you have an adroit and energetic mind you will find public affairs uninteresting; except in their occasional phases. If you have such a mind and must enter politics, hide it; otherwise democracy will distrust you. Whatever you do, be dull.

HIRAM WARREN JOHNSON

HIRAM JOHNSON

HIRAM JOHNSON would have enjoyed the French Revolution, if accident had made him radical at that time. He would have been stirred by the rising of the people; he would have given tongue to their grievances in a voice keyed to lash them to greater fury. He would have been excited by it as he never has been by the little risings of the masses which he has made vocal. In all the noisy early phases of it, he would have made the loudest noise. And he would have gone to the block when the real business of the revolution began with the fanatics at its helm.

In the Russian Revolution, he would have been a Kerensky; and he would have fled when the true believers in charge arrived. He is the orator of émeutes, who is fascinated by a multitude in a passion.

Johnson is not a revolutionary. Not in the least, not any more than Henry Cabot Lodge is. But revolution has a fierce attraction for him. He once said to me, speaking bitterly during the campaign, of Mr. Harding's prospective election, "The war has set back the people for a generation. They have bowed to a hundred repressed acts. They have become slaves to the government. They are frightened at the excesses in Russia. They are docile; and they will not recover from being so for many years. The interests which control the Republican party will make the most of their docility. In the end, of course, there will be a revolution, but it will not come in my time."

That "it will not come in my time" was said in a tone of regret. It was not so much that the Senator wanted revolution. I do not believe he did. But he wanted his chance, that outburst of popular resentment which would bring him to the front, with the excitement, the sense of power that would come from the response of the nation when his angry voice translated into words its elemental passion.

Turbulent popular feeling is breath in Johnson's nostrils. Twice he has thoroughly enjoyed its intoxication.

His political life was blank paper when the tumult of popular indignation swept California at the time Francis J. Heney, who was prosecuting the San Francisco grafters, was shot in the court room. He had thought nothing politically, he had felt nothing politically. He had neither convictions, nor passions, nor morals, politically speaking. He grew up in soil which does not produce lofty standards. Something of the mining-camp spirit still hung over California, which had been settled by adventurers, forty-niners, gold seekers, men who had left the East to "make a new start" where there was pay dirt. The State had a wild zest for life which was untrammeled by Puritanism. San Francisco had its Barbary Coast and in every restaurant its private dining rooms for women. Johnson himself was sprung from a father who was a "railroad lawyer," the agent of privileges in procuring special favors, by methods once well known, from the state legislature. The atmosphere of his youth was not one to develop a sensitive conscience or a high conception of public morals.

Johnson at this time was a practicing attorney, not noted for the quality of his community service. The administration of San Francisco had been a scandal for years. Few cared. It was a "corrupt and contented" city. The corruption grew worse. Lower and meaner grafters rose to take the place

of the earlier and more robust good fellows who
trafficked in the city o' shame. Graft lost class, and
lost caste. It was ultimately exposed in all its
shocking indecency. The light and licentious town
developed a conscience. Public indignation arose
and reached its height, when the grafters ventured
too far in the shooting of the attorney charged
with their prosecution.

Johnson then felt for the first time something he
had never felt before—the stirring of the storm of
angry popular feeling. It woke something in him,
something that he did not know existed before—
his instinct for the expression of public passion;
his love of the platform with yelling multitudes in
front of him.

He threw himself into the fray on the side of
civic virtue. The disturbance to the complacency
of San Francisco disturbed the complacency of the
State, which had calmly endured misgovernment
for many years. Misgovernment procured by the
railroad, the public utility corporations, the other
combinations of wealth, through their agents,
and through the corrupt politicians. Johnson
became the spokesman of public protest and the
reform governor of the State.

After that came battling for the Lord at Armageddon—the most intoxicating experience in American political history, for a man of Johnson's temperament. It was a revolution, not in a government, but in a party. Bonds were loosed. Immense personal enlargement came to those who had known the ties of regularity. It was an hour of freedom, unbridled political passion, unrestrained political utterance. Docility did not exist. Vast crowds thrilled with new hopes yelled themselves hoarse over angry words.

Association with Roosevelt on the Progressive ticket lifted Johnson from a local to a national importance. The whole country was the audience which leaped at his words. It was a revolution in tittle, a taste, a sample of what the real thing would be, with its breaking of restraints, its making of the mob a perfect instrument to play upon, its unleashing of passion to which to give tongue. Johnson has felt its wild stimulation and like a man who has used drugs the habit is upon him.

Moreover, his one chance lies that way. I have said that he is, by accident, radical. Let us imagine a great outburst of popular passion for reaction. And suppose that Johnson was, when it arrived, a political blank, as he was when Heney was shot. Johnson would have raised his angry voice against radicalism, just as readily as for it.

The essential thing with him is popular passion, not a political philosophy. He has no political philosophy. He has no real convictions. He does not reason or think deeply. His mentality is slight. He is the voice of many; instinctively he gives tongue to what the many feel; that is all.

Suppose the strong-lunged Californian were a political blank, just reaching the national consciousness, when the reaction against Wilson began and when the public swung to conservatism.

You know those vast tin amplifiers employed in big convention halls, or in out-door meetings, to carry the voice of the speaker to the remotest depths of the audience; Johnson is a vast tin amplifier of the voice of the mass. When the people had become "docile" he would have thundered "docility" to the uttermost bounds of the universe, if he had not by earlier utterances been definitely placed on the side opposed to docility.

But he had been definitely placed in the battle of Armageddon. A thousand ennuies located him for all political time. No convictions hold him where he is in case there be profit in changing sides; other men habitually conservative would have the preference over him on the other side. In this sense he is accidently radical, accidently because he happened to emerge in politics at a radical moment. That takes into account only the mental background of his political position. There is an element that was not chance. Public passion is almost invariably radical, springing as it does from the resentment of inequality, and Johnson is the tongue of public passion.

Is he dangerous? He is, only if public passion becomes dangerous and only up to the point where the speakers of revolution pass from the stage and the doers of it rig up their chopping blocks. At present he furnishes the words, the ugly words, which men throw instead of stones at the objects of their hate. He is the safety valve of gathering passion. Men listen to him and feel that they have done something to vindicate their rights. They applaud him to shake the roof, and vote for Mr. Harding.

It is customary to speak of his magnetism over crowds. He has no magnetism in personal contact. He walks toward you as if he were about to deliver a blow, an impression that is strengthened by his square menacing figure. His voice is unpleasant. His smile is wry. He not unusually has a complaint to make against the public, against the press, against fate, against you personally. He is not interested in people, as Roosevelt was to so an amazing degree, and as magnetic persons usually are. He is cold, hard, and selfish. His quarrels are numerous, with the campaign managers of the Armageddon fight, with his own campaign manager of 1920, with the newspaper correspondents. He is habitually pessimistic, and pessimism and magnetism do not go together.

His complaint that the people were docile and would not recover their confidence and self-assertion in his time, was a bit of his inevitable gloom. His dark habit of thought hung over his campaign for the presidential nomination of 1920, preventing his making a real effort in many states, and lay in the way of his success. He has few friends, love having been left out of his make-up. I do not speak of family affection—but love in its larger implications. Those who surround him—clerks and secretaries—have the air of repressed, starving personalities.

That which gathers the crowds and sets them shouting is not his magnetism but the perfect expression of their passion. For them and for it he is a sounding board. His voice with its hard angry tone, its mechanical rise and fall, has the ring of a hundred guillotines in operation. Having little culture, unintellectual, he is primitive as the mass before him. He talks their language and an instinct all his own gives him an exact sense of their emotions.

And what he says leaves the impression of tremendous sincerity. His sincerity does not arise from reasoned convictions but from hatred; deep and abiding hatred.

Senator Borah once said, "The difference between Johnson and me is that I regard questions from the point of view of principles while he regards them from the point of view of personalities. When a man opposes me I do not become angry at him. On the next issue he may agree with me. When a man opposes Johnson he hates him. He feels that the opposition is directed personally against him, not against the policy that separates them."

Johnson's opponents are the elements of reaction, the malefactors of great wealth, the supporters of that social inequality which the crowd resents. They stood in his path in California. They made impossible his nomination at Chicago. When the bitter enders, during the treaty fight, planned to send him on a tour of the country, these monied men closed their pocketbooks, exclaiming to Senator Knox, "What do you mean to do? Advertise this man Johnson and make him the Republican candidate for President? Not with our money."

Only the raising of a fund by Senator McCormick and some of the old Progressives, gave him his chance to speak. He hates them and when he attacks them it is with all the force and sincerity of his soul. It is no mere question of hatred, such as Roosevelt would employ to dramatize and make personal the issues he was representing to the people; it is bitter, revengeful detestation. It makes Johnson the most sincere man before the country to-day. And that pessimistic strain in his nature causes the darkness of his diatribe to seem all the more true.

But he swallows for expediency as other men swallow their convictions for it, and wrath is the bitterer dose. During the 1920 campaign he trafficked with Senator Penrose, the representative of hated wealth, for support at Chicago, offering, it has not been disclosed what considerations, for his aid.

He was ready at that time to take back his speech advocating the government ownership of railroads, a gesture against "the interests," made at the bidding of Hearst, at the beck of whose agents he is prone to bestir himself.

It must be an irksome livery, that of Hearst, for he hates all service and overshadowing. Equally irksome is his service to regularity under the rod of the Republican party. But he bows to it, and supports Harding whom he hates. He bobs up like a Jack-in-the-box and makes his laudatory speech whenever the name of Roosevelt comes up, though in his heart he must reverence none too deeply that overshadowing personality.

He has no roots except in the mob and no hope except in its aroused resentment against inequality. Not being interested in individuals he has not that personal organization possessed by Roosevelt, with his army of correspondents, friends and idolators, in every hamlet.

And of course he has little hope of ever controlling his party organization. He is curiously alone.

"There are only three men in the world whom I trust," he once said to a friend. There is no reason to regard this as an exaggeration. His attitude toward his associates in the Senate is this: "If I were crossing a desert with any one of them and there was only one water bottle, I should insist upon carrying that bottle."

On such pessimism and distrust it is impossible to build political success. It can come only when his pessimism and distrust coincide with like pessimism and distrust in the masses. He waits the day, but gloomily, without confidence.

PHILANDER CHASE KNOX

PHILANDER CHASE KNOX

"I LIKE Knox and I admire him tremendously, but I will not ask him to be my Secretary of State. He is too indifferent."

This characterization of the junior Senator from Pennsylvania, attributed to his late colleague President Harding, summarizes very aptly his strength and his weakness. One can very easily admire him and, when he drops the mask of dignity, which seems almost pompous in so diminutive a figure, one cannot help liking him. But in spite of his successes,—which his enemies attribute to luck, and he probably attributes to intellectual superiority,—he has never quite achieved greatness and will probably go down in history as one of the lesser luminaries in the political heavens.

Knox *is* indifferent, especially to those who do not know him intimately. It is not because he has been without ambition. On the contrary he has longed to soar like the eagle but he has the wings of the sparrow and whatever exertion he has made has ended in a feeble and futile fluttering.

I doubt if any man in public life has had so many honors thrust upon him. He has held three great offices of the Republic without so much as raising a hand for any of them. Unlike most men he did not travel the mucky road of politics to reach Washington nor compromise with circumstance to gain distinction. Three Presidents invited him to sit at their cabinet tables. Three times the Republican machine in Pennsylvania invited him to sit in the Senate. With graceful dignity he accepted all of these invitations not, indeed, unconscious of the fact that the selection in each case was a very happy one.

I do not mean by this that he is conceited. He is merely conscious of the fact that intellectually he is somewhat superior to his colleagues, most of whom, strangely enough, quite agree with him. They consult him and accept his counsel with almost childlike faith. To the mediocre politicians and provincial lawyers who constitute the bulk of the Senate and House of Representatives, he is a figure apart, who looks upon their antics with a kindly, but never amused, tolerance.

"I know nothing of politics," he said to me a

short time ago. "I have never been interested in politics as such."

This remark is rather enigmatical to the average member, who would, ordinarily, look upon the author as a dolt or pretender. They do not dare to do either in the case of Mr. Knox; therefore, the conclusion that he is indifferent. Never have the men associated with Mr. Knox questioned his capacity.

Robert Lansing, when he was Secretary of State, said of him; "Senator Lodge will not understand the treaty but he will fight for it for political reasons. Senator Knox will understand it thoroughly."

The observation seems almost prophetic in the light of what has since been disclosed. Mr. Lansing's faith in Mr. Knox's judgment seems to have been fully justified. I know of no one who has held more steadfastly the respect of colleagues in the Senate or at the Cabinet table, nor who has been more easily successful up to a certain point or so singularly unsuccessful beyond it. He has done valiant service for his country but he has failed lamentably to reach the heights from which he could look upon broader horizons.

In the early days of his career no one strove more whole heartedly. Destiny smiled upon him and the

White House seemed to beckon. He was not unaware of the opportunity nor was there anyone
more eager to grasp it. But he discovered that he
could not stir the enthusiasm that begets political
power. The secret, which enabled many other
men, many of whom he despised, to succeed, was
not his.

A temperamental dislike of the methods of politicians was followed by a strong animosity towards
those who crossed his political path and some of
those who went along beside it. He became hypercritical of those with whom he associated and
allowed a natural germ of cynicism to develop and
flourish within him. Little by little he has withdrawn from the active combat, a philosopher in
politics enamored of public life but unwilling to
suffer the inconveniences it involves.

It is no wonder then that his colleagues in the
Senate, especially the younger members, are somewhat in fear of the incisive tongue, for he wields it
frequently and contemptuously. When after his
election, Mr. Harding went South with Senator
Frelinghuysen, Senator Davis Elkins, and Senator
Hale, the older Senators, not, perhaps, without a
tinge of disappointment at having been left out,
marveled at the *entourage* the President had

selected for himself, but Knox was cynically un-disturbed.

"It is quite simple," he said, "I see nothing mysterious about it at all. The President wants relaxation—complete mental relaxation."

No less biting was his comment on Robert Lansing when that gentleman started on the high road of public service as Counselor of the State Department. The bandy-legged messenger who guards the door of the Secretary of State is the negro, Eddie Savoy. Eddie, in his way, is a personage. For forty years he has ushered diplomatists in and out of the Secretary's office; his short bent figure gives the only air of permanence to an institution which seems to be in a constant state of flux. When the Lansing appointment was announced Mr. Knox observed: "I would as soon ask Eddie Savoy an opinion on foreign affairs as Robert Lansing."

The roots of Mr. Knox's superciliousness dip down deep into the relationships begun a score of years ago. To understand him as he is it is necessary to understand him as he was when his career was before him. William McKinley asked him to become Attorney General in his Cabinet. He was then forty-two years old, a political nobody. What reputation he had was confined to Pittsburg and a selected few of the steel millionaires in Wall Street, but among the selected few were names to be conjured with, such as Andrew Carnegie and Henry C. Frick. Whether President McKinley's interest in Knox was spontaneous or prompted by Mr. Frick I do not know. Mr. Knox likes to believe that Mr. Frick did not enter into the equation. Mr. Knox declined, saying that he could not sacrifice his lucrative practice but that in four years he would accept the invitation if the President cared to renew it.

It was renewed. At the age of forty-six, Mr. Knox quit the bar for politics, or, as he would say, statecraft. His appointment evoked a storm of protest from such immaculate journals as the New York *World*. They dubbed him, "Frick's man," and predicted that the Department of Justice would be turned into a Wall Street anteroom for the convenience of the capitalistic combinations then flouting the Sherman anti-trust law. The charges, of course, were as wide of the mark as most of the ebullitions of the yellow journals.

Mr. Knox began his public career by attacking the Northern Securities merger, against the judgment of some of the highest-paid lawyers of the country. The Supreme Court sustained him. It was the greatest victory the government ever won under the Sherman law. Thereafter Mr. Knox, who had been labeled a corporation lawyer, was proclaimed a trust buster. By the time he was fifty he had become the greatest Attorney General in a half century. Certainly the mark he set has never been reached by any of his successors.

When Mr. Roosevelt came into the White House Mr. Knox was at the pinnacle of his career and was as much admired by his new chief as by his martyred predecessor. In ability Mr. Roosevelt considered him next to Elihu Root,—for which Mr. Root was never quite forgiven. It is generally known that President Roosevelt believed that Mr. Root was the best qualified man in the country to succeed him, but at the same time, being an astute politician, he knew that he could not be elected. His attitude to his Secretary of State was the same as Senator Lodge's toward himself, when he said in 1920: "I know that I would make an excellent President, but I realize that I would make a poor candidate."

Root being out of it because of this obvious defect, President Roosevelt proceeded to groom Mr. Knox for the nomination. Mr. Knox at the President's suggestion, prepared and delivered several speeches in the hope that he would awaken popular enthusiasm. The attempt failed dismally.

There was not a responsive throb, not even a vague echo. Mr. Knox knew that he possessed not the merest shred of the leadership necessary to a presidential candidate.

He went back to the Senate, where he had succeeded Matthew Quay upon his resignation from the Cabinet, sadder if wiser, while William H. Taft draped upon his broad shoulders the mantle of Roosevelt.

Mr. Knox has never quite recovered from that disappointment, but he did not altogether abandon hope. He accepted a place in the Taft Cabinet as Secretary of State, more for the opportunities it offered than for the pleasure of the associations, for Mr. Knox's attitude toward President Taft was never more than passive tolerance tinged with contempt. This new venture was no more successful than the old. He made it quite evident that a new régime was to be established in the State Department. The policies originated by John Hay and developed with singular brilliancy by Mr. Root were shunted into the background and a new era was proclaimed. It is unnecessary to comment on the dismal essay at "dollar diplomacy" and the

Mexican policy of that period. The simple fact
is that Mr. Knox's name is not associated with a
single successful foreign policy. Some might have
succeeded but unfortunately the energy displayed
at the outset of his career in this new field was soon
dissipated. Mr. Knox disliked the methods of
diplomacy. He lacked both the patience and the
finesse. He went to the Department, over which
he was supposed to preside, but rarely. For weeks
at a time Washington saw nothing of him. The
administration of the Department was left largely
to Huntington Wilson, whose ineptitude was
colossal.

Fortunately for Mr. Knox the extent of his
failure was somewhat screened from public view
by the dust and clatter of the collapse of the Taft
Administration, but it left its mark on him. He
had failed dismally to eclipse his predecessor, Elihu
Root. He had eliminated himself from all consideration as one of the very great statesmen of his
period. He was a bitterly disappointed man. Not
only his associates but the members of the diplomatic corps were made to feel the sting of his resentment against overwhelming circumstances.
Such references as that directed at the French
Ambassador, M. Jules Jusserand, now dean of the

diplomatic corps, whom he called "the magpie," cost him many friends.

Upon the inauguration of President Wilson Mr. Knox slipped quietly away to Valley Forge. Public life, however, still had for him its attractions, and when Senator Oliver retired, he returned to the Senate. During the war his great talents were dormant. He merely came and went, a curious little detached figure apparently quite unresponsive to the emotions which swept the country during that eventful period.

With the signing of the armistice he aroused himself from his apparent torpor. Although he was quite without feeling during the stress and storm, the situation created by the presentation of the Treaty of Versailles with its interwoven League of Nations stirred his intellectual interest. He became the leader of the little band of "irreconcilables" who girded their armor to prevent what they regarded as a catastrophic sacrifice of American interests. At the same time Mr. Knox narrowly missed another opportunity to lift himself conspicuously above the heads of stump speakers who, for the most part, to-day comprise the Senate.

During that memorable fight Senator Lodge incurred the enmity at one time or another of every faction in the Senate. He could not be trusted to maintain the same position over night, shifting as expediency demanded until most of his colleagues, particularly the irreconcilables, were exasperated beyond endurance. At one of the most critical periods Senator Borah appealed to Senator Knox to wrest the leadership from the Massachusetts Senator, with intimations that he would have the support of the "bitter enders" at the forthcoming convention at Chicago. Mr. Knox does not love Mr. Lodge but he refused to consider the proposal. He was indifferent. His last great political opportunity went glimmering.

As I have said Mr. Knox can be very charming but I doubt that he sincerely admires any of the public men with whom he has been associated, or can call any of them, from the purely personal viewpoint, his friends, with the possible exception of Andrew Mellon, whom he caused to be appointed Secretary of the Treasury. Of course, he likes many of his colleagues, after a fashion, especially those who admire him, but that is another matter. The intimacy usually implied in the term friendship does not enter into such relations.

For some of the more important men he has known, he has shown a very distinct dislike. It is

ROBERT LANSING

ROBERT LANSING

HE who believes in luck should study the career of Robert Lansing. Mr. Lansing probably thinks that the goddess of chance played him a scurvy trick, after having admitted him to the Olympian heights, to break him as suddenly as she made him.

Robert Lansing's real misfortune was not knowing how to play his luck. It is curious the fear men have of death. The former Secretary of State's only hope of immortality was to commit political suicide, and he lacked the courage or the vision to fall upon his sword.

When Woodrow Wilson was elected President for the first time he appointed Mr. Bryan Secretary of State. The opinion Mr. Wilson entertained of Mr. Bryan we all know. Mr. Wilson was not given to letting his thoughts run wild, but on one occasion, with pen in hand, he permitted himself the luxury of saying what he thought and expressed the pious hope that somebody would knock the distinguished Nebraskan into a cocked hat and thus dispose of the perpetual candidate who was the Old Man of the Sea to the Democratic Party.

Circumstances alter cases; Mr. Wilson as a private citizen could say and think what he pleased; as President he was compelled to make Mr. Bryan Secretary of State. As Mr. Bryan knew nothing of history and less of European politics and had a superb disdain of diplomacy—diplomacy according to the tenets of Bryanism being an unholy and immoral game in which the foreign players were always trying to outmaneuver the virtuous and innocent American—he was provided with a political nurse, mentor, and guardian in the person of John Bassett Moore, who had a long and brilliant career as an international lawyer and diplomatist. Mr. Bryan busied himself with finding soft jobs for deserving Democrats, preaching and inculcating the virtues of grape juice to the diplomatic corps, and concocting plans whereby the sword was to be beaten into a typewriter and war become a lost art. Meanwhile Mr. Moore was doing the serious work of the Department.

No two men were more unlike than Mr. Bryan and Mr. Moore; Mr. Bryan a bundle of loosely tied emotions to whom a catchy phrase or an unsound theory is more precious than a natural law or the wisdom of the philosopher; Mr. Moore an intellect who has subordinated his emotions, and to whom facts are as important as mathematics to an engineer. It was an incompatible union; it could not last. Mr. Moore became impatient of his chief's vagaries and, about a year later, returned to the dignified quiet of Columbia University.

This was early in 1914. Now for the random way in which chance weaves her skein. Mr. Moore went out of the Department and left the office of Counselor vacant, an office, up to that time, so little known that the public, if it gave the matter any thought, believed its occupant was the legal adviser of the Department, while, as a matter of fact, he is the Under Secretary, which is now the official designation.

At this stage of his career Mr. Lansing was connected with the Department as an adviser on international affairs and had represented the United States in many international arbitrations. He was known to a small and select circle of lawyers specializing in international law, but to the public his name meant nothing. He had always been a good Democrat, although he was married to the daughter of the late John W. Foster,

215

who wound up a long and brilliant diplomatic life as Secretary of State in President Harrison's Cabinet after Mr. Blaine's resignation.

Mr. Lansing had made Washington his home for many years, and when the new Democratic Administration came into power he believed his services to the party entitled him to recognition, and he sought the appointment of Third Assistant Secretary of State. The Third Assistant Secretary is the official Social Secretary of the Government. When royalty or other distinguished persons come to this country as the guests of the nation the Third Assistant Secretary is the Master of Ceremonies. He has to see that all the forms are properly complied with and nothing happens to mar the visitors' enjoyment; he sends out invitations, in the name of the State Department, to the funerals of Ambassadors or the inauguration of the President. But for some reason Mr. Lansing's praiseworthy ambition was defeated.

Mr. Moore had knowledge, learning, and experience, but he was denied the gift of divination. Had he known that a few months later a half crazed youth in an unheard of place was to be the unconscious agent to set the whole world aflame, undoubtedly he would have put up with Mr. Bryan's curious ideas and peculiar methods and stuck to his desk at the State Department, and Mr. Lansing would never have been heard of. But at the turning point in Mr. Moore's career his luck deserted him and Mr. Lansing became the beneficiary. Mr. Lansing, who would have been satisfied with the appointment of Third Assistant Secretary of State, a minor place in the hierarchy, was appointed by Mr. Wilson Counselor of the Department of State.

The appointment created no excitement. In March, 1914, foreign affairs had little interest for the American people. There was Mexico, of course, and Japan; there were the usual routine questions to form the customary work of the department; but the skies were serene; murder, rape, and sudden death no one thought of; Lloyd's, which will gamble on anything from the weather to an ocean tragedy, would have written a policy at a ridiculously low premium on the maintenance of the peace of Europe; any statesman rash enough to have predicted war for the United States within three years would have aroused the concern of his friends and the professional solicitude of his physician. Apparently Mr. Lansing had tumbled into an easy and dignified post which would not unduly tax his physical or mental strength. He could congratulate himself upon his good fortune.

A few months later the situation changed. The State Department became not only the center about which the whole machinery of the Government revolved but on it was focused the attention of the country and the thoughts of Europe. The Counselor of the Department was lifted out of his obscurity; despatches to the belligerents signed "Lansing" were published in the newspapers, statements were issued by him, he was interviewed; he received Ambassadors, and when an Ambassador visited the State Department the nerve centers of the whole world were affected. Again, a few months later, in June, 1915, Mr. Bryan kindly accommodated Mr. Wilson by knocking himself into a cocked hat, and Mr. Lansing was appointed Secretary of State. Few men had risen so rapidly. He had no reason to complain of his luck.

Mr. Wilson made some extraordinary appointments—a close observer has said he could read motives but not men—and his appointment of Mr. Lansing at a time of crisis would have been inexplicable were it not logical as Mr. Wilson reasoned. Mr. Wilson did not invite as his asso-

ciates his intellectual equals or those who dared
to oppose him; it was necessary that the State
Department should have a titular head, but Mr.
Wilson was resolved to be his own Secretary of
State and take into his own hands the control of
foreign policy. No great man, no man great
enough to be Secretary of State when the world
was in upheaval, would have consented to that in-
dignity; no man jealous of his own self-respect
could have remained Mr. Wilson's Secretary of
State for long. A Secretary of State or any other
member of the Cabinet must of course subordinate
his judgment to that of the President, for the
President is the final court of appeal. But Mr.
Wilson went further than that; he heaped almost
unparalleled affront upon Mr. Lansing; he made
the great office of Secretary of State ridiculous,
and he invested its incumbent with no greater
authority than that of a copyist.

Perhaps Mr. Wilson reads men better than his
critics believed; perhaps Mr. Wilson had fully
taken the measure of Mr. Lansing and knew how
far he could go.

Nature never intended Mr. Lansing to be a
leader of men, to fight for a great cause, or to en-
gage in physical or intellectual combat. His life

has been too soft for that, and he is naturally indolent. He is fond of, and has more than the amateur's appreciation for, music, painting, poetry, and the classics of literature. He has dabbled in verse, he sketches and he has written, but without brilliancy. Accident made him a lawyer, but he was really intended to be an artist; he would have produced no masterpiece, for genius is not in him, but he would have been happy in his work and perhaps have given inspiration to men of greater talent. Without being a fanatic or dogmatic, he is strongly religious; religion to him has a meaning and is not merely a convention; he has a code which he has always observed and ideals which he has preserved; he is charitable in his judgments and has never allowed his prejudices to influence his actions; he is, to use a word so often misapplied, a gentleman, and his motto is *Noblesse oblige*. Typical of the standard he sets for himself was the admirable restraint he showed after his abrupt dismissal from the Cabinet. He neither sought vindication through the newspapers, nor posed as a victim, nor soothed his feelings by denunciations of the President; he did not make a nuisance of himself by inflicting the recital of his grievances upon his friends or hinting darkly at revelations.

He kept quiet and went about his affairs as a gentleman should.

Why, it may be asked, should a man with so many fine qualities have cut such a sorry figure? The answer perhaps is that he suffers from the defects of his qualities, fine as we must admit them to be; too fine, perhaps, for a coarser world.

When a weak and somewhat easy-going man, immensely pleased with his own exalted position, has to deal with a man of iron will, ruthless in his methods, he is necessarily at a disadvantage. Considering Mr. Lansing's temperamental defects and the effect of his training, his failure is no mystery.

Until Mr. Lansing became Secretary of State he had never known responsibility. Practically his entire life had been spent as a subordinate, carrying out with zeal and intelligence the tasks assigned to him, but always in obedience to a stronger mind. Nothing more weakens character or intellect than for a man habitually to turn to another for direction or inspiration; always to play the part of an inferior to a mental superior. For years Mr. Lansing had been connected with many international arbitrations which, theoretically, was a magnificent training for a future Secretary of

State, and actually would have destroyed the creative and administrative usefulness of a much stronger man than Robert Lansing.

In the whole mummery of international relations there is nothing more farcical than an international arbitration. It is always preceded by great popular excitement. A ship is seized, a boundary is run a few degrees north or south of the conventional line, something else equally trivial fires the patriotic heart. The flag has been insulted, the offending nation is a land grabber, national honor must be vindicated. Secretaries of State write notes, ambassadors are instructed, the press becomes rabid, speeches are made; the public is advised to remain calm, but it is also assured there will be no surrender. After a few weeks the public forgets about the insult or the way in which it has been robbed; but the responsible officials who have never allowed themselves to become excited, continue the pleasing pastime of writing notes.

Months, sometimes years, drag on, then a new Secretary of State or a Foreign Minister, to clean the slate, proposes that the childish business be ended by an international arbitration. More weeks, more often months, are spent in agreeing upon the terms of reference, and finally the dispute goes before an "impartial arbitral tribunal." Both sides appoint agents and secretaries, an imposing array of counsel, technical experts; and as the counsel are always well paid they have a conscientious obligation to earn their fees.

More months are required to prepare the case, which frequently runs into many printed volumes; and the more volumes the better pleased everybody is, as size denotes importance. The arbitrators, although they are governed by principles of law, know what is expected of them, and they rarely disappoint. Almost invariably their decision is a compromise, so nicely shaded that while neither side can claim victory neither side suffers the humiliation of defeat. As by that time both nations have long forgotten the original cause of the quarrel their people are quite content when they are told the decision is in their favor. As junior counsel Mr. Lansing's name appears in many international arbitrations, and it was precisely the work for which he was fitted.

If Mr. Lansing had been a man of more robust fiber, he would have returned his portfolio to Mr. Wilson as early as 1916, for the President was writing notes to the belligerents and did not, even as a perfunctory courtesy, consult his Secretary of

State; he made it only too patent he did not consider his advice worth asking. Mr. Lansing was too fond of his official prominence to surrender it easily, and that is another curious thing about the man. Somewhat vain, holding himself in much higher estimation than the world did, few men have so thoroughly enjoyed office as he. But he remained the quiet and unassuming gentleman he had always been; and he certainly could not have deluded himself into believing that there was a still higher office for him to occupy.

Mr. Lansing could not screw up his courage to resign in 1916. The following year the United States was at war and he naturally could not desert his post; but in 1919 Mr. Lansing was given another opportunity, and still he was obdurate. He has told us in his public confession that he tried to persuade the President not to go to Paris. Mr. Wilson, as usual, remained unpersuaded, and Mr. Lansing humbly followed in his train.

Then, of course, Mr. Lansing could not resign, but in Paris he was even more grossly humiliated; he was completely shut out from the President's confidence; he wrote letters to Mr. Wilson which the President did not deign to answer; so little did Mr. Lansing know what was being done that he sought information from the Chinese Delegates! It sounds incredible, it seems even more incredible that a Secretary of State should put himself in such an undignified position, and having done so should invite the world to share his ignominy. But he has set it down in his book as if he believed it was ample defense, instead of realizing that it is condemnation.

Curious contradictions! One might expect a sensitive man, a man who has never courted publicity, who has none of the genius of the self-advertiser, to crave forgetfulness for the Paris episode, to shrink from publicly exposing himself and his humiliations, but Mr. Lansing seemingly revels in his self-dissection. The President slaps his face; in his pride he summons all the world to look upon the marks left by the Executive palm. He feels the sting, and he enters upon an elaborate defense to show it is the stigmata of martyrdom. A treaty was framed of which he disapproved, yet he could sign it without wrench of conscience. Unreconciled to resignation in Paris, he returned to Washington as if nothing had happened, again to resume his subservient relations to the President.

Opportunity, we are told, knocks only once at a

man's door, but while opportunity thundered at Mr. Lansing's portal "his ear was closed with the cotton of negligence."

Early in 1920 Mr. Wilson dismissed him, brutally, abruptly, with the petulance of an invalid too tired to be fair; for a reason so obviously disingenuous that Mr. Lansing had the sympathy of the country. He should either have told the truth then and there or forever have held his peace; and had he remained mute out of the mystery would have grown a myth. The fictitious Lansing would have become an historical character. But he must needs write a book. It does not make pleasant reading. It does not make its author a hero.

It does, however, answer the question the curious asked at the time of his appointment: "Why did the President make Mr. Lansing Secretary of State?"

BOIES PENROSE

BOIES PENROSE

THE most striking victim of the American propensity for exaggeration is the senior Senator from Pennsylvania, Boies Penrose. He has a personality and contour that lend themselves to caricature. Only a few deft strokes are needed to make his ponderous figure and heavy jowl the counterpart of a typical boss, an institution for which the American people have a pardonable affection in these days of political quackery. For, when the worst is said of the imposing array of bosses from Tweed down to the present time, they could be forgiven much because they were what they were. That is why, perhaps, the altogether fanciful picture of Penrose, propped on his pillows with his telephone at his bedside directing the embattled delegates at Chicago, who in sheer desperation turned to Warren G. Harding, is dwelt upon fondly by a deluded public.

Penrose does not despise the appurtenances of

bossism. If the truth were told he probably likes the idea of being represented as the hard-fisted master of party destinies. He knows that such a reputation inspires awe if not respect, on the part of the rank and file, from the humble precinct worker to the gentleman of large affairs who provides the necessary campaign funds. It has its value, sentimental as well as practical, for the American people likes to set up its own political idols. The politicians who for the moment guide the destinies of the nation are so misdrawn, so illuminated with virtues and endowed with vices quite foreign to them, that they frequently achieve a personality quite fictitious, but which, none the less, passes current in the popular mind as genuine.

Nothing could be more grotesque, for example, than the picture of Senator Smoot, who is merely a sublimated messenger boy, as one of the arbiters of the Republican policies; or of Senator Lodge, by sheer strength of leadership, restraining the discordant Republican elements in the Senate from kicking over the traces. This is journalist "copy" written for a popular imagination which finds the truth too tepid.

Boies Penrose serves the purpose of appeasing

national appetite for what the magazine editors call "dynamic stuff."

But the real Boies Penrose is not all as he is pictured. At a cursory glance he might appear to be a physiological, psychological, and political anachronism. At least he is sufficiently different from his colleagues to be, if not actually mysterious, not easily understandable. There is something fundamental about him. He inspires a certain awe which may not be magnetic but has the same effect upon those who surround him; where he sits is the head of the table.

I doubt if Lodge or Knox or Hughes could ever fathom the secret of his power; they are not cast in the same mould. His colleagues smile at his idiosyncracies—behind his back—but they approach him with the respect due to a master. Many of them admire him, not a few hate him, but all of them fear him. It is rather a singular thing that Senator La Follette, himself at the pinnacle of his championship of the Wisconsin progressive idea, was probably on friendlier terms with the senior Senator from Pennsylvania than any of the other leaders of those reactionary forces with whom he was tilting. He knew where Penrose stood and it is not at all improbable that behind the Penrose reticence there was a modicum of admiration for the methods of the redoubtable little colleague, who in his way, was a more inexorable boss than Penrose himself ever dreamed of being. The mutual understanding was there, even if it never became articulate.

Penrose has peculiarities which put him in a niche quite his own. He eschews conversation as an idle affectation. He dislikes to shake hands, preferring the Chinese fashion of holding his on his own expansive paunch. When he finds it necessary to talk at all he speaks the precise truth as he sees it without consideration for the feelings of those he happens to be addressing. The results are frequently so ludicrous, particularly when he enters a colloquy on the Senate floor, that he is given credit for a much more pronounced sense of humor than he actually possesses. I doubt that he is always conscious of the element of humor and I suspect that if he realized that his observations were to evoke laughter he would deliberately choose a less satirical or flippant method of expression.

This temperamental characteristic was illustrated by an episode in the Senate chamber not long ago. Penrose, entering, found his chair oc-

cupied by a Democratic colleague who had over-
estimated his capacity for the doubtful stuff that
is purveyed in these days of Volsteadism and whose
condition was apparent to everyone on the floor
and in the galleries. Penrose is, perhaps, the most
widely known personage in the Senate. His tower-
ing figure makes him conspicuous. But the most
of the myriads of trippers who visit the Capitol.
do not know one senator from another. They
rely for identification upon little charts showing
the arrangements of the seats on the floor each one
of which is labeled with a senator's name.

Now Penrose, might or might not have suspected that these trippers following their charts,
would pick out the snoring recumbent figure as
his own. He decided to remove all possibility of
error and addressing the chair with usual solemnity
said, "Mr. President, I desire the chair to record
the fact that the seat of the senior Senator from
Pennsylvania has not been occupied by himself
at the present session. It is occupied by another."
The galleries roared; the somnolent Senator
shambled over to his own side of the aisle and
Senator Penrose was given credit, by the unwise,
for humor quite unintended.

Life with Mr. Penrose is a much more serious

business than most people imagine. And it became even more serious a little while ago when illness laid hold of him and his brother, a physician, prescribed dietary rules restricting the freedom that he had once exercised without restraint. There was something lion-like in the gaunt figure in the rolling chair which he occupied when he returned to the Senate from his sick bed. It was amazing that he recovered; it was even more amazing that he should have submitted to the rigorous rules laid down by his doctor, even if that doctor was his own brother. The bated breath with which Pennsylvania politicians awaited bulletins from his bedside was a striking acknowledgment of the power he wields.

The evolution of Boies Penrose is an amusing commentary upon American politics in more ways than one. Three years after he was graduated from Harvard College he was elected to the Pennsylvania State Legislature on a reform ticket. His election was made the occasion for great rejoicing on the part of the good people of Philadelphia. And well might they rejoice. They had at last driven a wedge into the sinister political machine that had brought the city of brotherly love into disrepute as a boss-ridden municipality.

Their young leader had wealth, which has its advantages, and social position, which to a Philadelphian is as dear as life itself. Moreover he had ability and all that makes for success. His fame as a reform leader spread throughout the land and across the seas. James Bryce, in his first edition of his *American Commonwealth* cited him as an example of the sterling type of young Americans who were arousing themselves at that time to rescue the municipal and state governments from the grip of the vicious boss system.

In the subsequent editions of the *American Commonwealth* you will find no reference to Mr. Penrose. Something had happened to him and to the reform movement. Whether he was struck by a bolt from the heavens or a bolt from Matthew Stanley Quay is immaterial. The fact is that after a few years' residence in Harrisburg, the seat of the government of the commonwealth of Pennsylvania, he counseled with himself and solemnly decided that Providence had never selected him to be the apostle of the political millenium.

Most men are born radicals and die conservatives. The development is gradual and represents the result of years of experience. But Penrose

He has raised it whenever he has had the opportunity to do so, but not for the reason assigned.
He is no man's tool. The suggestion that Boies
Penrose personally has ever profited financially
through politics is too absurd to be entertained for
a moment. Of course, he expects the interests,
whom the party serves with tariff protection, to
save the party at the polls and they usually do so.
But that in the opinion of the senior Senator from
Pennsylvania is the essence of sound politics.

Unbelievable as it may sound in these days,
Senator Penrose actually thinks that most men
are dependent for their daily bread upon the success of a very small group of financiers, magnates,
or whatever you care to call the great leaders of the
world of business.

Years of experience has convinced him that
the human race is composed, for the most part, of
hopelessly improvident people and that a great
part of the globe would be depopulated through
starvation and disease if it were not for the foresight, ability, and thrift of the handful of leaders
whom Divine Providence has provided. He looks
upon himself as one of the instruments of Providence and he sincerely believes that the policies
which he has supported since his early experience

with the reformers are responsible for the happiness and prosperity of many a family. He would consider it the height of absurdity for any of these poor, worthy, but ignorant people to expect the comforts which they have enjoyed without the protection afforded their employers by the Republican Party.

By this somewhat unpopular method of reasoning, he believes that he of all the men in public life has made the most persistent and consistent fight for the masses. It is undoubtedly this calm faith and sincere belief in his own rectitude which has enabled him to hold the tremendous power he has exerted since Nelson Aldrich retired from the Senate.

I have presented his political philosophy in some detail because he is probably the most misjudged man in Washington. People are inclined to look upon him as a glorified boss who deals in politics as other men deal in commodities;—it is hardly a fair estimate of the man. He considers himself the chosen leader of the most intelligent people of a great commonwealth who is rendering tremendous service to the country. I do not agree with that estimate either. But taken all and all it seems to me that the country owes him a debt of gratitude for having been sincere when another course would have been more profitable. It is a relief to find one at least who has never been called a hypocrite.

Senator Penrose does not hate Democrats; he does not consider them important enough for that; he merely despises them. They are to his mind an inferior class of human beings who should not be intrusted with the affairs of the nation. Reformers irritate him. They are either self-seeking hypocrites or deluded. In neither case has he the time nor inclination to listen to their suggestions or heed their maledictions.

He had an abiding hatred for Theodore Roosevelt when he was in the White House, but he supported him loyally so long as he was the leader of the Party. When Colonel Roosevelt bolted the hatred ran the last gamut. He was classed as an arch criminal for having smashed the organization.

Penrose is an enigma to those who know him only casually, especially those who view life through the rose glasses of culture. They marvel at the extent to which he has been able to dictate to men who appear to be his superiors. I have heard him called a cave man by some, by others a boor; but he is neither. He observes the amenities of life so far as they are necessary, but only so far. He is impatient of mediocrity; he will not tolerate stupidity and he loathes hypocrisy. I would not say that he has bad manners; he has none at all.

Throughout the recent eclipse of the Republican Party, which began with the Roosevelt default, no member remained more steadfast than the Pennsylvania leader. He accepted the inevitable and bided his time like the politicians of the old school of which he is one of the few conspicuous surviving examples. Expediency does not enter into his make-up; he made no effort to keep himself in the limelight, for he is by the Party, of the Party, and for the Party.

Now that the Party is back again, in power, more than one of his colleagues suspect that Penrose, if his health permits, will emerge from the background as the real leader of the Senate majority. His political past is against him. But he knows men and his tutelage under Aldrich has not been forgotten.

WILLIAM EDGAR BORAH

WILLIAM E. BORAH

TAKEN at its best, life, to William E. Borah, is little more than a troublesome pilgrimage to the grave.

This does not mean that he is a misanthrope or a seer of distorted vision. On the contrary his sympathies are broad and he has an elusive charm, more apparent in the early years of his political career than now. But, for some reason, probably temperamental, he is in the habit of dwelling upon the dangers that beset the republic—dangers which are sometimes very real. Nevertheless an hour in his presence is more often than not depressing; it leaves one with a sense of impending calamity. There are few bright spots on his horizon.

It is not altogether to his discredit that his more venerable colleagues look upon him as a young man—he is fifty-six; nor does it imply merely arrested political development. For all of his pessimism he maintains a certain freshness, if belligerency, of spirit which is puzzling not only to those who have long since accustomed themselves to the party yoke but to those whom experience has taught the art of compromise. For Borah hates the discipline that organization entails, in spite of his respect for organization, and he dislikes compromise however often he is driven to it.

This may be accounted for by the fact that he was not obliged to fight his way laboriously upward on the lower rungs of politics—he landed in the Senate from an Idaho law office in one pyrotechnical leap when he was only forty two—and by the fact that in his make-up he is singularly unpolitical. Disassociating him from his senatorial environment it is much easier to imagine him as a devotee of academic culture, a university professor, a moral crusader, even a poet, than as a politician.

There is in his make-up an underlying Celtic strain which may account for his moodiness, his emotionalism, and his impulsiveness. These characteristics are constantly cropping up. For many years he has buried himself in a somber suite of rooms in the Senate office building as far away from his colleagues as he could get. There he lives in an atmosphere of academic quiet. There he reads and studies incessantly, far from the maddening crowd of politics. This detachment has probably bred a suspicion that marks his actions. He has no intimates, no associates who call him "Bill." He is not a social being. He is rarely seen where men and women congregate. He is virtually unknown in that strange bedlam composed largely of social climbers and official poseurs called Washington society. He neither smokes, drinks, nor plays. What relaxation he gets is on the back of a western nag in Rock Creek Park where he may be seen any morning cantering along —alone. He does not ride for pleasure; his physician ordered it and it is a very businesslike matter. If he experiences any of the exhilaration that comes to men in the saddle he contrives to conceal it.

On the floor of the Senate he is quite a different person. There his unmistakable genius for oratory is given full sweep and when he speaks his colleagues usually listen, not because they agree with what he says but because they are charmed by the easy and melodious flow of his words. There is a hint of Ingersoll in his speeches which are full of alliteration and rhythmic phrases. He has a sense of form sadly lacking in his stammering and inarticulate colleagues, for oratory in the Senate is probably at its lowest ebb. But, strangely enough, it is only occasionally that he makes a lasting impression. His eloquence ripples like water and leaves scarcely more trace.

Mr. Borah's entire political career has been characterized by an impulsiveness which has given him a halo of popularity but has never enabled him to garner the fruits of plodding labor. At one time or another this has led him to break with nearly every faction with which he has been identified. The "regular" Republicans have felt that they never could rely upon him; the "progressive" element has found him inconstant and at intervals he has threatened to pull down the party house of the Republicans and to bring destruction to one or other of the leaders whom he dislikes.

This was illustrated by an observation he made to me one spring morning in 1919 when the Republican attitude toward the League of Nations was still in the formative process. Borah was "convinced" that Elihu Root and Will H. Hays were conspiring to induce the Republicans to accept the League and he said, quite seriously, that he had about come to the conclusion that it would be necessary to wreck the Republican Party to save the country. Root, he told me, was pro-British to the last degree and Hays, he said, was cajoled by the great international bankers who trembled at the delay of peace.

"If such men are to lead the Republican Party," he declared, "the sooner it is destroyed the better."

Of course, he did not take the stump. He has failed so often to carry out his threats of rebellion that they no longer inspire the fear they once did. Although he has repeatedly turned against the organization he has managed to escape being an outlaw. This singular trait of political conservatism came conspicuously into play in 1912 when Roosevelt turned upon the machine. All through the stormy days of that stormy Chicago convention Senator Borah could be found at the side of that one leader for whom he had a consistent regard. He was with him up to the very last moment before the die was cast. He was almost successful at the eleventh hour in inducing Mr. Roosevelt to abandon his mad project. They were closeted together on the evening of the clamorous meeting of the progressives in a hotel across the street.

"We have come to the parting of the ways, Colonel," Borah said to his chief. "This far I have gone with you. I can go no further." He urged Roosevelt not to take the step which would mean the disruption of the party and defeat. Roosevelt wavered. But before he could reach the decision Borah sought a committee from the outlaw meeting, burst into the room, and enthusiastically announced that the stage was set for the demonstration that was to mark a new political era.

Roosevelt, hat in hand, turned to Borah and said, "You see, I can't desert my friends now." The ex-President went his way and Borah came back to the old Republican fold.

From that time to this he has followed his own way which, fortunately for the Republican Party, has been within organization limits, but his relations with his fellows are neither intimate nor serene. Some of the Republicans, who can be forgiven for not understanding a man who re-respects neither party decrees nor traditions, feel that Borah is so American that he possesses one of the characteristics of the aboriginal Indian—in other words, that he is cunning, that he will not play the game according to organization rules. He has a habit of making too many mental reservations. I am not quite sure that these allegations could be supported before an impartial tribunal. I am rather inclined to the belief that to maintain his position in the Senate Borah has had to become a shrewd trader.

Fortunately for himself he is too much of a personage to be ignored or suppressed, and manages to be a power in a party which has no love for him.

He is virtually a party to himself. He cannot be controlled by the ordinary political methods. His constituency is small and evidently devoted to him and his state is remote; he is not compelled to do the irksome political chores that cost Senators their political independence. However doubtful he might be as a positive asset his dexterity and power of expression are such that he would be very dangerous as a liability. A report that Borah is on the rampage affects Republican leaders very much as a run on a bank affects financial leaders. They are not quite sure when either is going to stop. Borah knows that most of the men with whom he is dealing are clay and estimates with uncanny accuracy the degree to which he can compel them to meet his demands.

This method has not always been successful. It was singularly unsuccessful in the case of Senator Penrose. Borah is the antithesis of Penrose, whom he dislikes intensely. Several years ago he interpreted a remark made by the Senator from

Pennsylvania to another Senator as a thrust at his own political ethics, or lack of them. It was a petty affair at most and Penrose never admitted the accuracy of Borah's construction, but Borah has had nothing to do with him since. When the present Congress was in process of organization Borah announced that he would bolt the party caucus if Penrose were slated for the chairmanship of the Finance Committee to which he was entitled according to the rule of seniority. It was a ticklish situation. The Republicans had a bare majority in the Senate and if any of them deserted the organization it might mean Democratic control. The leaders were disturbed and tried to mollify the defiant Senator from Idaho with every means at hand even giving assurance that the Senator from Pennsylvania would vote against the Peace Treaty and the League of Nations which was supposed to represent his vital interest at that time. He refused to compromise and announced that Penrose must go. He was offered every committee assignment that he or his friends wanted, and accepted them, but as a matter of right.

Penrose was determined not to be displaced to satisfy what he regarded as a colleague's whim. He sat silent in his office receiving reports from hour to hour on Borah's state of mind. On the day before the caucus Borah whispered that he intended to make charges against the Pennsylvania leader that would provide a sensation regardless of any effect they might have upon the party or the country. The report was brought to Penrose. Instead of trembling he sent word to Borah that he might say what he pleased concerning his political career but that if he made any personal charges he would regret them to his dying day. Borah appeared to understand. He did not even attend the caucus and Penrose was duly elected. Whether he was trading for committee assignments or initiated the fight on political grounds is a question he alone can answer, if anyone should have the temerity to ask it.

The same violence of his likes and dislikes is shown in his attitude toward the British and his espousal of the Irish cause. At the time of the visit of the British mission to Washington, Vice-President Marshall designated Senator Borah a member of the committee appointed to escort the British visitors into the chamber. This Borah resented as a personal affront.

"Marshall has a distorted sense of humor," he said. "He knows I dislike the British and that I despise the hypocrite Balfour." This feeling was probably due in large measure to the Irish lineage which Borah can trace in his ancestry as well as a temperamental dislike of the British methods of maintaining control over subject peoples.

It is difficult to label Senator Borah from a political standpoint. His most striking characteristic is his inconsistency. For a long time in the early days of the progressive movement he displayed a marked inclination to be "irregular" and he is to be found voting for most measures for which the "progressives" claimed sponsorship, but when the more radical leaders began to advocate the recall of the judiciary, Borah rose up and delivered an invective the memory of which lingers in the Capitol. It was one of the few speeches he has made that had a permanent effect and, strangely enough, it was the kind of speech that might have well been delivered by Root or Knox.

There has always been reason to believe that Borah was never more enamored of La Follette in his prime, or of Hiram Johnson, than he has been of the "reactionary" leaders with whom he has been oftentimes in open conflict. When the latter deluded himself with the hope of securing the Republican nomination, Borah was supposed to be his chief supporter. When Johnson had eliminated Lowden and Wood, and seemed to have eliminated Harding, Borah showed more interest in the Knox candidacy. He wanted Knox at the head of the ticket mainly because he knew that Knox was an implacable foe of the League of Nations. On that fateful Friday night in Chicago when the signs of the trend toward Harding had begun to appear, the Senator from Idaho was anxious and prepared to place Knox's name in nomination and begged Johnson to swing his delegates in that direction.

Borah has succeeded very well in concealing his own ambitions, possibly because he is more cautious than some of his impetuous colleagues, or because the opportunity has never come for an avowal. But among those who have followed his career there is a very strong suspicion that his one great desire was to be the successor of Roosevelt. This might be one reason for his antagonism toward the politicians of the old régime, such as Penrose, who have barred his way in that direction, and his fitful devotion to progressivism championed by others. The failure to realize this ambition might account in some measure for his later reticence and his suspicion of politicians in general. He has shown a pronounced distrust of them. The only exception has been the audacious Ambassador to the Court of Saint James who in his *Review* and in his *Weekly* flattered the Senator from Idaho with an absence of restraint that might have made a more trusting person skeptical.

The Senator from Idaho has too many years before him to justify predictions concerning his career. Whatever faults he might have they do not entirely obscure his virtues. It is possible that the occasion might arise for him to serve as the spokesman of a popular cause, which he would do with undoubted earnestness and eloquence, in which event he might still become a dominating figure in American politics.

A Selection from the
Catalogue of

G. P. PUTNAM'S SONS

❧

**Complete Catalogue sent
on application**

The Mirrors of Downing Street

By "A Gentleman with a Duster"

8vo. With 12 Portraits

A selection from a host of reviews of an amazing and brilliant volume:

"Since Lytton Strachey shocked and amused us by his *Eminent Victorians*, no book written by an Englishman has been so audacious, so reckless, so clever, and so full of prejudices, apparently based on principles."—Maurice Francis Egan in the *New York Times*.

"Of fascinating interest, with a style pungent and epigrammatic . . . does not contain a dull line . . . there is scarcely one of the great controversies which agitated British political waters during and since the war that is not touched on . . . the author is partisan in his friendships, and he is a good hater, so his work is altogether engaging."—*New York Herald*.

"A very serious book, without being heavy, a daring work, without being reckless. It is judicial in tone, endeavoring to give each man his due, setting down naught in malice or partiality . . . a work of keen interest and highly illuminating."—*Cincinnati Times-Star*.

"This book of scintillating wit and almost uncanny power of vivid phrase-making."—*N. Y. Evening Mail*.

"Some of his characterizations fairly take one's breath away. His epigrams are as skillful as those of 'E. T. Raymond,' and his analysis is reminiscent of Lytton Strachey. . . . This book has created a sensation in England, it will create another in America."—*News-Leader, Richmond, Va.*

"It is a book that every intelligent person should read, dispelling, as it does, a number of the illusions to which war conditions have given birth . . . the book is one to be read for its light on specific facts and on individual men. Often the author's least elaborated statements are the most startling . . . it is written with the vim and audacity of Lytton Strachey's *Eminent Victorians*, and it has in addition a very vivid news interest, and it is just both in its iconoclasm and in its frank hero worship—of the right heroes."—*Chicago Post*.

"It is one of the few cases of a startling work being also a fine piece of literature . . . the author is obviously on the inside. No merely imaginative person could have produced such a picture gallery."—*N. Y. Evening Telegram*.

"One of the most interesting studies that has been presented to English or American public."—*Troy Record*.

New York   **G. P. PUTNAM'S SONS**   London

AT THE
SUPREME WAR COUNCIL

By

CAPTAIN PETER E. WRIGHT

Late Assistant Secretary, Supreme War Council

8 Portraits

"A Literary Blast Which Shook All England"

It will shake America, too, these revelations whose author knew the intimate records and, as interpreter, participated in the conferences of those overlords of the Great War, the Supreme War Council members.

World secrets are bared and great reputations crumpled. Idols of Britain and of France, Haig, Robertson, Maurice, and Pétain are pictured as creatures of clay with Repington abetting their sorry projects. The illusion of Allied numerical inferiority is shattered. Superior in numbers almost always, the Allied inferiority lay in generalship alone (before Foch), says the author.

Captain Wright lifts the veil. Logic, statistics, and apparent proof substantiate his statements. Whether right or wrong, wise or otherwise, certainly he is fearless. "If my charges are false," he says, "let them sue me for libel. Then all the facts will come out!"

G. P. PUTNAM'S SONS

New York   London